GINGER ROGERS

GINGER ROGERS

A Pyramid Illustrated History of the Movies

by
PATRICK McGILLIGAN

General Editor: **TED SENNETT**

PUBLICATIONS
NEW YORK

For Mother and Father

GINGER ROGERS
A Pyramid Illustrated History of the Movies

Pyramid edition published December 1975

ISBN 0-515-03894-6

Library of Congress Catalog Card Number: 75-18546

Printed in the United States of America

Pyramid Books are published by Pyramid Communications, Inc. Its trademarks, consisting of the word "Pyramid" and the portrayal of a pyramid, are registered in the United States Patent Office.

Pyramid Communications, Inc., 919 Third Avenue, New York, N.Y. 10022

(graphic design by ANTHONY BASILE)

ACKNOWLEDGMENTS

Special material contributed by Debra Weiner

Susan Dalton and the staff of the Wisconsin Center for Theatre Research; University Film Center in Cambridge, Massachusetts; Barry Brown and Gerald Peary; Marc and Fran Weiner; William K. Everson; my editor, Ted Sennett, for his long-distance advice; Films Incorporated; Macmillan; Audio Brandon; and the companies that made and distributed the films of Ginger Rogers: Paramount Pictures Corp., RKO Radio Pictures, First National Pictures, Warner Brothers, Inc., Twentieth Century-Fox Film Corp., United Artists, Columbia Pictures, Metro-Goldwyn-Mayer, Inc., British Lion Films, Bill Sargent Productions, and Golden Eagle Productions.

Photographs: Jerry Vermilye, The Memory Shop,
Gene Andrewski, Movie Star News, Cinemabilia,
Quality First, and Penguin Photos

CONTENTS

"You bring out a lot of your own thoughts and attitudes when acting. I think a great deal of it has to do with the inner you. You know, there's nothing damnable about being a strong woman. The world needs strong women. There are a lot of strong women you do not see who are guiding, helping, mothering strong men. They want to remain unseen. It's kind of nice to be able to play a strong woman who is seen."

—Ginger Rogers

INTRODUCTION: THE ART OF BEING GINGER

She stirred the heart rather than the mind: charming, always charming.

"Ginger has become an American favorite—as American as apple pie—because Americans can identify with her," mused an anonymous writer for *Life* magazine in 1942, at the zenith of her career. "She could easily be the girl who lives across the street. She is not uncomfortably beautiful. She is just beautiful enough. She is not an affront to other women. She gives them hope that they can be like her. She can wise-crack from the side of her mouth, but she is clearly an idealist. Her green eyes shine with self-reliance. She believes in God and love and a hard day's work. She is a living affirmation of the holiest American legend: the success story."

On the cover of the magazine, in a photograph so beguiling that it is worth the while of dreamers to look it up, is Ginger Rogers, née Virginia Katherine McMath, in tumbling russet hair, a T-shirt, and rubber hip boots, grasping a fishing rod.

Hers was a physical quality at heart: svelte, ageless, inviting, plain but fancy. She was the woman with schoolgirl eyes and a vanilla smile. She was the woman who somehow combined an old-fashioned look with a hep-cat style. Though, from movie to movie, from character to character, she varied her countenance—assuming a pony-tail, bubble cut, pompadour, page-boy or pig-tails, modifying the color or length and, most importantly, the effect of her hair-do—she never spoiled the basic cheerleader appeal.

It seems scarcely incidental that her memory, for movie buffs, is sharpest as the able partner of Fred Astaire in those ten lustrous films they danced through together. She contributed equally to their hyphenated achievement. She was self-taught but instinctually balletic, in her gestures, however small, as well as her bounding leaps. There was a glow and definition and ease to her movement that

perfectly suited their partnership. A gay, seemingly effortless performer—with characteristically splashing arms —she brought something loose, ragged and ingenuous to comparison with Astaire's smooth, cultured control.

But though it may be fashionable to remember her solely as one-half of the screen's most famous dancing duo, it is unfair to relegate her name to brief mention in the annals of film history. For she was a solo actress of considerable talent and dimension, underrated in the passage of time even as she was overrated during her own reigning epoch. Before she teamed with Astaire, fully one-third of her career had already been consummated and, after their split, fully another third, comprising her most interesting appearances in films, was logged.

Few actresses—perhaps Barbara Stanwyck or, in a minor vein, Joan Blondell—had her astonishing versatility or, rather, her splendid opportunities to display that range. Rogers flitted easily from the Astaire dance epics to light tragedy (such as *Stage Door*) to light comedy (such as *Bachelor Mother*), with appropriate interludes for fluffy material, rarely compromising her believability. She starred in few actual blockbusters, true, and few actual "classics," besides the Astaire films. She acted in more than her share of shlock, yes, but also in a raft of minor opuses that look better and better with each viewing. Her legacy, writ large in the public eye via seventy-three motion pictures, is uneven but respectable.

Among her arsenal of types were the stenographer, the fast-order waitress, the hatcheck girl, the newshound, the office clerk and, repeatedly, the chorine, flapper, actress, or star. That, incidentally, is not only the canon of a particular actress but also the occupational profile of an entire, "socialized" sex. So was her tremendous popularity any wonder? In that single, recurrent calling (of chorine to star) was silently expressed the aggregate ambitions of a multitude of women trying to escape or forget the forced conditions of their lives. Rogers played the pretense (a showgirl of sorts in nearly thirty movies) on the screen and reflected the fabled American "success story" in her real life. She also mirrored that "success" in her imagined movie-life, since, as time passed, she became a fashion-magazine editor (*Lady in the Dark*), an attorney (*The Groom Wore Spurs*) and, again and again, a movie star. Literally and figuratively, she worked her way out of the kick line.

Curiously, fantastically, whatever her humble circumstances, she never seemed the worse for wear: impeccably well-dressed through-

out her career, even though she was normally cast as a breadwinner. Audiences swallowed logic wholesale to see, again and again, a struggling chorine garbed in lavish furs or smart, backless dresses or elegant hats. It didn't matter; it was all part of the doting game. Once named by dress designers as "best exemplifying the dress dictates of the typical American girl" (in *Fortune* magazine of May, 1938), Ginger Rogers was clothes-conscious for the term of her public life, and to view her movies is to glimpse a fashion parade of chic American styles over the last decades. There is a certain irony in the fact that she, who often dressed privately in expensive Paris designs by Grès, Saint Laurent, and Givenchy, became a fashion consultant to the J. C. Penney chain in 1972.

Yet her glamour was peculiarly homegrown, and so was her virtue. Despite her worldly-wise air, she expressed a native morality in contemporary fabric, which is why, perhaps, she only graced one "period" film, Frank Borzage's *Magnificent Doll,* in which she (poorly) impersonated Dolly Madison. She was rarely the heel (coming nearest in *Black Widow*), flirting with the distinctions of the moral code only at the beginning of her career, before the contours had sharpened, and at the lingering conclusion, when fewer and fewer roles drifted her way. She only "died" once, in *Upper World,* for death would be too loathsome for a player with so much vitality, so much goodness, and so many followers. Tears—and there is, invariably, a heart-tugging moment in many of her movies in which she weeps unashamedly at some outrage—indicated not simply her integrity as an actress but also her vulnerability (her violated innocence) as a character. Except for a few quirky pictures in which Hollywood's predilection for exploring Freud is given sway, she was a clean soul, an honest jane, a next-door girl, silks and jewelry notwithstanding.

For, in vehicles which spanned nearly four decades, Rogers always played, in the words of critic Otis Ferguson, "the girl." She posed the romantic foil in her attractive youth and, even in her middle age, in films like *Forever Female* and *Black Widow.* Invariably, she found her screen existence entangled with the presence of a male. That was her curse (not hers alone) and, oddly, also her blessing, for she converted those ordinary circumstances into fame, fortune, and a credible sweetheart persona. She gave life to the type: she cracked wise, she talked sense, she worked her own schemes. If she was traditional and old-fashioned, sometimes to the cloying brink, then she was also as honest in her characters' emotions as could rightfully be

expected of any envoy from Hollywood.

And by her canny resilience, Rogers nearly subverted the clichés of movieland romance. Usually single and often happily so, she invariably resisted the romeo until the final script-contrived clinch; even then, typically, she would flee under mistaken pretenses, only to be retrieved in the last moments by a chastened lover. When, especially in early roles (such as *Professional Sweetheart* or *Chance at Heaven*), she lobbied fiercely for a husband, it was usually to the detriment of the script or the virtual collapse of the movie. She wasn't exactly sexless but neither was she exactly a *femme fatale.** She never played the siren or enchantress. There was something safe and platonic and self-effacing about her character that was actually exploited for comedy purposes in two movies about unconsummated love, *Fifth Avenue Girl* and *Lucky Partners.* She was more tomboy than love child. It is hardly surprising, then, that her male co-stars (such as David Niven in *Bachelor Mother* or Dennis Morgan in *Kitty Foyle*) often provided a pale and tedious contrast to so free-flying a woman.

*During the filming of the dance for "Jenny" in *Lady in the Dark,* director Mitchell Leisen asked the actress to be "sexier" with bumps and grinds, but Rogers staunchly demurred, contending that such gymnastics would "hurt her image." Leisen was forced to resort to hidden cameras for the desired effect, according to *Hollywood Director* by David Chierichetti.

Though marriage (for Ginger Rogers) always seemed an improbable concession to convention, scenarists frequently conspired to pronounce the sacred vows anyway. She was only truly "married" on a few occasions (notably in *Tender Comrade* where she served as faithful surrogate to a generation of war wives) and on those few occasions the union was customarily quarrelsome (*We're Not Married*), static (*Monkey Business*), crumbling (*Black Widow*), already dissolved (*Teenage Rebel*), or an excuse for upward mobility (*Once Upon a Honeymoon*). She was much too strong-willed, really, to be subjected to such ordinary domestic "bliss." And, in one delightful, eccentric, and unusual film, *Tom, Dick and Harry,* she savagely lampooned this entire boy-girl business by dangling three misty-eyed romeos at arm's length for the story's duration. How interesting, then, that the private Ginger Rogers had a similarly fitful relationship to men: she had five marriages—all torrid, all rather brief.*

Age never seemed to daunt her

*The men in Ginger Rogers' life literally deserve a footnote, for they fared poorly with, in the words of Lloyd Shearer, this "driving, confident, domineering, highly-opinionated perfectionist." They were: vaudevillian Jack Culpepper, whom she married in 1928 and divorced in 1931; actor Lew Ayres (1934-1940); actor Jack Briggs (1943-1949); actor Jacques Bergerac, who became spouse four in 1953 and lasted until 1957; and her current husband William Marshall, whom she married in 1961.

though, in truth, her career declined, like that of most actresses, when the ingénue and soubrette roles, Hollywood's regrettable staple, no longer suited her. In the 1950s, she was consigned to playing characters founded on previous type. Usually, she was cast as an aging actress or star, the grown-up version of her youthful chorine roles. Generally, she was discerning enough to choose (and fortunate enough to be offered) vehicles which exploited her past "experience" as a celluloid showgirl in an intelligent manner, so that she neatly capitalized on her bygone allure. Her matronliness became a pun; her past in the cinema, whether as Astaire's partner (*The Barkleys of Broadway*) or as an imaginary siren of the silent era (*Dreamboat*), became a wry observation on her present situation. Only in two instances, *Monkey Business* and *Teenage Rebel,* did she depart significantly from stock, playing, in the former, a research chemist's wife, and in the latter, an emotion-torn divorced mother, and these were among the best movies of her waning decade.

The irony in this tinsel-town pigeon-hole is that Ginger Rogers never really withered, as the studios expect and demand of their femme players. She aged slowly, imperceptibly, gracefully, staying radiant and beautiful and, yes, youthful well past her supposed prime. The unconscious irony, for example, of a film like *Forever Female* is that Rogers—of whom character after character remarks upon her supposed physical decline—looks ravishing and behaves with her usual juvenile bounce. There was something about this actress, something in the core of her popularity, which suggested the eternal verities of youth.

That is why, surely, her best-remembered movies capitalize on this childlike quality and, especially, those deft vignettes of kiddie behavior which she performed so well (and parlayed, memorably, into Swedish garble in *Bachelor Mother*). It was a trait she had cultivated since vaudeville when her standard routine had included "recalations about the anumals, including Mama Nyceroserous and Papa Hippopapumis." Two of her best projects, Billy Wilder's *The Major and the Minor* and Howard Hawks' *Monkey Business,* divide evenly into moments of hard-headed maturity and flashes of precocious youth. There was always a hint of giddiness under that spruce composure. She could look childish, even at middle-age, and she could behave like a child dexterously on cue, as if a split personality. It was a silly, shallow quality, but she made it captivating.

But she was no child in the contractual arena, though she was always a daughter: Her "positiveness and dogmatic independence," from all accounts, were "either inherited or acquired" from her mother, Lela Rogers, the wiry, indefatigable, near-legendary "stage mother" who molded and propelled Rogers, Jr.'s career. Lela once estimated that only "a fortune-hunter or a worthless good-for-nothing or some ambitious schemer" would marry a motion-picture star, and it is recorded for posterity in the actress' divorce proceedings that mama acted divisively on her feelings.* Mama was not only mama but family and counsel as well. Lela herself led a fascinating life: she fought her first husband in court for custody of Ginger, became a scenarist for Fox Studios, served in perpetuity as her daughter's business manager (reportedly garnering 20 percent of the star's earnings) and eventually (partly, the story goes, to leaven her interference on the sets of her daughter's movies) held a supervisory position in the New Talent School at RKO where she was reportedly instrumental in the careers of Jack Carson and Lucille Ball.

Mama Lela achieved brief notoriety in her middle years for her testimony before the House Un-American Activities Committee and her membership in the super-patriotic Motion Picture Alliance. She fingered Clifford Odets (for his humanistic *None But the Lonely Heart*) and scenarist Dalton Trumbo as Communists and even claimed that daughter Ginger had refused, in Trumbo's script for *Tender Comrade*, to exclaim: "Share and share alike—that's democracy!" The line was supposedly assigned to another actress. Hardly a political sophisticate, Lela went too far when, in 1947, on ABC radio nationwide, she labeled a Broadway-bound property called *The Gentleman from Athens* "communistic" because it concerned the adventures of a corrupt congressman. She was promptly sued for one million dollars and the case was settled handsomely out of court.

They, mother and daughter, were inseparable; and it would be as foolhardy to estimate their intimacy as it would be to underestimate the impact of the relationship. It was common knowledge in the screen colony, for example, that when "Leelee" and "Geegee," as they fondly referred to themselves, had a crucial decision to make, business or careerwise, mother ultimately made the choice. Lela betrayed herself in their many "joint" interviews by reverting to the editorial "we." In the middle of these press confabs, according to one contemporary account, Lela would be prone to interject, "Now, be quiet, Ginger; you don't know what this is all about," and Ginger would re-

*Lloyd Shearer, "One of the World's Most Fascinating Women," *Parade* magazine, April 9, 1961.

join with a sigh, "There you have the capsule history of my life." For the unschooled, untrained, "fatherless" actress, it was to be the formative influence in her career, accounting for much that was both feminist and traditional in her filmography.

Advised by Lela, Ginger Rogers became one of the most willful, motivated, and calculating actresses ever to haggle over subclauses; that is the ready explanation for much of what is exciting, unpredictable, and often contradictory in her screenland career. She showed sharp-minded acumen early on by free-lancing often (in a breadth of roles, with a range of studios) and by signing a long-term contract subsequently with RKO. From all accounts, she wearied of her Astaire partnership at the same time as Astaire, and ventured forth solo. That courage and initiative led to her period of highest creativity in the late thirties and forties.

A story is told, illustrating her brashness, of a single-minded Ginger Rogers determined to land the role of the Queen of England in John Ford's *Mary of Scotland*. She pleaded, cajoled, and even tested for the role in make-up and affected voice; but she was nixed (the role went to Florence Eldridge, wife of star Fredric March), and one studio executive supposedly exclaimed, "Hell! Nobody'll know it's her and if they do know, they'll keep waiting for Queen Elizabeth to crack wise or get up and do a number!" It took her success with Astaire, and her commensurate box-office allure, to convince RKO otherwise, and to open the door to such movies as *Stage Door* and *Kitty Foyle*. Her freelancing in the forties, which also had its element of daring since it occurred at the height of her prowess, may have been part grudge, part revenge, but it was most assuredly well-advised. The dividends of her iron attitude were a career which straddled the modes of comedy, melodrama, and musical, never imprisoned or delimited by one or the other.

Over the years, she toyed with the idea of establishing her own production unit, and finally, in 1964, achieved that ambition with her mounting of the barely-released *The Confession*. She had directorial ambitions, too, which she never surrendered. "I think I'd be a good director for certain types of pictures," she said in 1953. "I'd even like to direct a remake of *Kitty Foyle*. My experience should make me valuable, not as I was when I danced with Fred Astaire, but as a different kind of performer with a different kind of usefulness." The plans never materialized, alas, and the possibilities are only conjecture. Since World War II, after all, only one woman, Ida Lupino, and she mainly in the television field, has flourished behind

With mother Lela on the set of THE MAJOR AND THE MINOR (1942)

the camera in Hollywood. The name of Ginger Rogers joins a list which includes Claudette Colbert, Hedy Lamarr, Bette Davis, and other women whose executive ambitions were stymied by a male-exclusive Hollywood.

But audacity and drive, however admirable, are not wisdom, and her career judgment was not spotless. She was one of the many actresses, for instance, who rejected the choice role of Hildy Johnson in Howard Hawks' hilarious remake of *The Front Page, His Girl Friday,* for reasons lost to posterity. After her phenomenal success in *Kitty Foyle,* the actress was also sought for the honky-tonk girl in *Ball of Fire,* another Hawks picture, produced by Sam Goldwyn. She turned the role down, however, on the grounds that she wanted to play only ladies. Goldwyn reportedly exclaimed: "You tell Ginger Rogers for me that ladies stink up the place!" And, according to mother Lela's testimony before HUAC, daughter Ginger also declined a role in *Carrie,* the film version of Theodore Dreiser's *Sister Carrie,* for the preposterous reason that it was "open propaganda."

This narrow, conservative, and hygienic opinion of herself predictably led to further and further retreat from Hollywood, and less and less filmmaking until, after 1965, she totally scorned the craft. By the late 1960s, she had restricted herself entirely to summer stock, dinner theater, substitute star for *Hello, Dolly!,* and touring attraction for *Coco.* In the case of the latter property, she unexpectedly encountered acid-age morality in the script and made a public gambit of refusing to utter the sole four-letter word in the play. Long a Republican, ever a devout Christian Scientist, she, who had been so central to the mass sensibility of two decades in America, was already distanced from her industry in 1956 when, on the occasion of the filming of *The First Traveling Saleslady,* she extolled "family" pictures such as *Bachelor Mother, Kitty Foyle, Fifth Avenue Girl* and *Having Wonderful Time,* while decrying "this juvenile delinquent *Blackboard Jungle* kind of thing." She told Hedda Hopper: "That's the sort of thing that does the industry harm. Oh, of course, they may be considered artistic triumphs among intellectuals, but that isn't the group where the money comes from. They couldn't fill the New York Metropolitan Opera House more than once." Note: It was roughly one decade before the real flood tide of sex, violence, and profanity.

But that is why her image, her memory, is nostalgic, rooted in the past. Fixed in the consciousness of the nation is the recollection of an instinctual, artless actress—an

engaging singer-dancer, a light tragedienne and a sprightly comedienne—of redoubtable gifts. A word about those gifts: Her skill was of a very practical, and practicable, strain. Mimicry, especially, was her forte, and there are golden glimpses of this knack, such as her "Anytime Annie" masquerade in *42nd Street.* She was fluent in the external details of life, such as fashion or slang or even the womanly handling of a cigarette, surface qualities which endeared her more understandably to the moment than to the future. She was an earthbound character whose favorite domain was the sidewalk: she cultivated the raised eyebrow, the street jargon, the knowing tone.*

Yet her small contribution to Americana is a lasting one, and Ginger Rogers is nowadays being happily restored to her deserved place in the American cinema, in books such as Molly Haskell's *From Reverence to Rape* and Marjorie Rosen's *Popcorn Venus.* For she was a strong, resourceful, and enchanting heroine of the ilk which seems nearly and sadly extinct. Her bequest is largely escapist, true, mainly diverting, not only in the glorious Astaire-Rogers musicals which flourished anachronistically during the bitter Depression, but also in the many happy-go-lucky, even-tempered vehicles she toplined alone. Such movies not only gave pleasure but, understandably, by their lavish unconcern, they exuded ferocious irony too. She only starred in one movie, after all, *Storm Warning,* that deigned to deliver a social comment, and that during the spiraling dip of her career in 1950.

Yet she somehow transcended prim little categories. She survived her often-dismal filmic environment with miraculous, but still human, agility, and she juggled the traits which always threatened to restrict her to formula and cliché. Lapses of sheer embroidery intermingled with moments of seeming genius. The synthetic and the sanguine struggled with the genuine and the restless. One element crashed against another in the person of Ginger Rogers, and in the still-resounding reverberation, filmgoers can discern an artist of insight, talent, and honesty.

*A situation which was cerebral evidently troubled her, as *Lady in the Dark,* with its florid psychoses, awkwardly proved. In those psychoanalytical scenes on the couch, director Mitchell Leisen recalled before his death, "She didn't know what the hell she was talking about. I'd go in quietly and try to explain to her what the thing meant and pull it out of her. I mean I really pulled."

THE EARLY YEARS

Some brief facts about the legend: Virginia Katherine McMath was born on July 16, 1911, in Independence, Missouri, and received her illustrious nickname, Ginger, from a cousin who, as a child, was unable to pronounce Virginia. Baby Ginger led an admittedly raucous infancy. She moved to Texas with her parents at an early age, was subsequently "kidnapped" by her father in the midst of divorce proceedings, and ultimately ended in the arms of Lela in Kansas City where, not yet five, she appeared in a few long-lost advertising films. Mama McMath became a scenarist for Baby Marie Osborn vehicles, and the two shared a brief residency in New York City where Lela, according to later studio publicity, inexplicably refused to allow Ginger, then six, to perform in a George Walsh picture in progress at Fox Studios in Fort Lee, New Jersey. Mother and daughter returned to Texas where Lela served as drama critic for the Fort Worth newspaper, manager of a local symphony orchestra and, during her spare hours, composer of playlets concerned with Texas history. Thirteen-year-old Ginger starred in onesuch, *The Death of St. Dennis*, at Fort Worth Central High School in 1924.

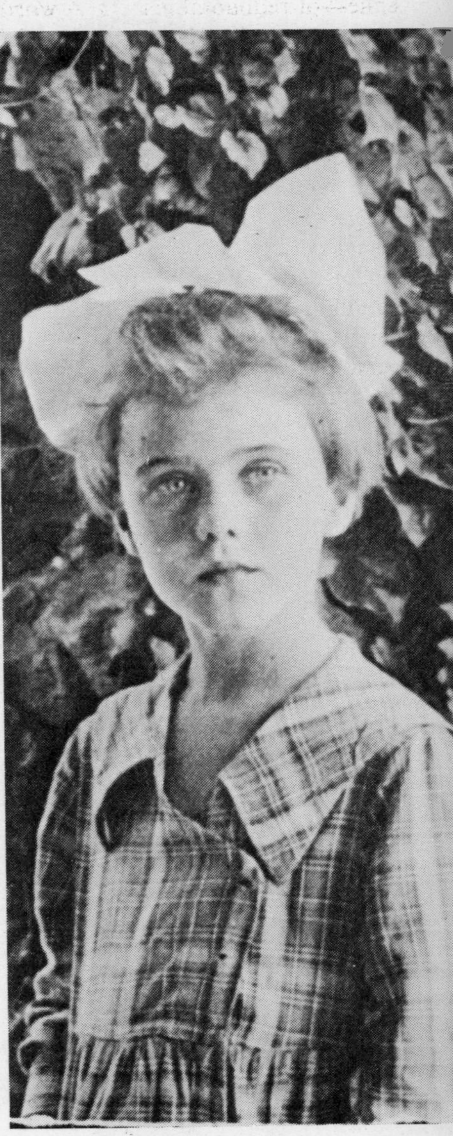
Young Ginger

One week in 1925, Ginger substituted for a dancer in the act of vaudeville top-liner Eddie Foy, when he played the Fort Worth

On Broadway in GIRL CRAZY (1930)

area; but her real chance arrived in January of 1926 when the teen-age aspirant entered a statewide Charleston contest in Dallas. Wearing a white crepe dress with countless rhinestones, devised in collaboration with Lela, she copped first prize, winning a month-long booking on the Texas-Oklahoma circuit. This led circuitously to a three-year stint on the road in the Midwest and the South, with Ginger becoming a regular, eventually, on the Paramount-Publix chain in musical revues. She toured, during these days, with Eddie Lowry and his band, comedian Willie Howard, and Paul Ash and his orchestra. In 1929, importantly, she was signed for the new musical comedy, *Top Speed*, by tunesmiths Bert Kalmar and Harry Ruby, a property which played Broadway to favorable reviews and friendly word-of-mouth. *Variety* tabbed Ginger as "a likely comedienne for future musicals" although "facial grimaces, when dancing, make her look not unlike Fanny Brice." Also espying the budding soubrette, so the story goes, was Paramount producer Walter Wanger, who was in the opening-night audience and promptly signed Rogers to a contract with the studio.

Thus began, somewhat modestly, the initial period of her screen career, in which she mostly served an inauspicious apprenticeship but, significantly, honed her capabilities and garnered a deserved reputation as a dependable (and likable) performer. She had actually appeared in several short subjects during her vaudeville days: *Campus Sweethearts,* with Rudy Vallee; *A Night in the Dormitory,* a twenty-minute item with two songs handled by Rogers; and *Office Blues*. But now began headlong activity; in less than three years, she would work in twenty motion pictures, over one-fourth of her entire output. They were a heady mix too: simpering melodramas, banal romantic comedies, and mainly flaccid musicals. Before her fated teaming with Astaire in *Flying Down to Rio* in 1933, she served time as the good-natured foil to such effervescent comics as Joe E. Brown, Ed Wynn, Charlie Ruggles, and Jack Oakie in movies that, but for one or two exceptions, are overwhelmingly silly.

Her first five vehicles were shot at the Long Island studios of Paramount, during spare time and after-midnight hours, since she performed nightly in *Top Speed* and, later, George Gershwin's *Girl*

CAMPUS SWEETHEARTS (1930). A short with Rudy Vallee (standing)

Crazy (a musical which boasted Ethel Merman belting "I Got Rhythm"). *Young Man of Manhattan,* her debut feature, concerned a sportswriter (Norman Foster) who falls in love with a columnist (Claudette Colbert). The tale, directed by Monta Bell, himself an ex-newsman, lightly explored the tension which arose between an ambitious husband and his successful wife, but included such improbable complications as blindness caused by Scotch and the advances of a flapper. Rogers was the flapper, naturally, a modernist named Puff who pursued the sports flack and also warbled two ditties, one entitled "I've Got 'It,' But 'It' Don't Do Me No Good." Hardly earth-shaking stuff, but Rogers nevertheless made a small impact with her line, "Cigarette me, big boy!" which enjoyed a trendy vogue nationwide. And, in this first lunge at posterity, she exuded a certain rough poise and raw promise, looking slim and youthful (she was only nineteen) in fashionably short, curly hair.

Slightly better, if equally ridiculous, was *Queen High,* next on her agenda in 1930, directed by Fred Newmeyer, once in Harold Lloyd's stable. It was also a musical (containing songs such as "I Love the

YOUNG MAN OF MANHATTAN (1930). With Charles Ruggles and Norman Foster

Ladies In My Own Peculiar Way," sung by Charlie Ruggles), revolving around the bickering of two partners in the garter business, played by Frank Morgan and the erstwhile Ruggles. To end their longstanding feud, both draw cards to determine who shall act as butler for the other. Rogers enters into this nonsense as a niece who effects a reconciliation between the two curmudgeonly businessmen, as well as neatly firming her romance with Stanley Smith. But, regrettably, again she was plot embroidery, fleetingly seen, and the movie glides along solely on the wacky portrayals by Morgan and Ruggles.

More corn: *The Sap from Syracuse,* next in 1930, was based on a play that flopped grandly on Broadway. Jack Oakie, whose specialty was broad comedy and a dumb leer, played H. Littleton Looney, a crane driver who is the butt of practical jokes. Looney, which also describes the plot, is somehow convinced that he is the engineer of a new "Erie Canal" and thus begins a voyage to France, marked by shadowy intrigues and utter absurdity. Again, Rogers fills a small role, playing the heroine of the debacle who sings one duet with Oakie and then melts into the background. She was still exaggerated in her acting manner, in

QUEEN HIGH (1930). As Polly Rockwell

THE SAP FROM SYRACUSE (1930). With Jack Oakie

keeping with the awkward histrionics of the early sound age. *The New York Times* wrote: "She is pretty and does very well by things as they are."

Ed Wynn, the "Perfect Fool," made his "talkies" debut—and Ethel Merman made her feature screen debut—in *Follow the Leader,* Rogers' final Paramount release in 1930. A taste for Wynn's bubbly theatrics is necessary to enjoy this tall tale of a meek "gangster" (a case of mistaken identity) who is commanded by his cohorts to kidnap a show queen (Ethel Merman), enabling her understudy (Ginger Rogers), the gang's favorite, to substitute in the limelight. Some pleasantly asinine gags ensue: Wynn kidnaps the wrong chorine, namely Rogers; he then poses as the salesman of an inventive lock which plays "The Star Spangled Banner" when tinkered with, forcing patriotic burglars to stand erect, salute, and be captured; and he accidentally chloroforms himself during the hectic climax. Rogers, though second-billed, again performed minor romantic love digressions (opposite the constant Stanley Smith) in a pleasing if unsubstantial performance. Mediocre, but light, goofy, and smoothly directed, *Follow the Leader* is a film whose inanities were more endearing then, during Wynn's heyday, than now.

Best of her Paramount period was *Honor Among Lovers,* unobtrusively directed by Dorothy Arzner, Hollywood's most active (and virtually only) woman director, whose elegant, sophisticated, and feminist films are being revived with growing appreciation today. Director Arzner herself spotted Rogers in *Girl Crazy* (where one of her songs was "Embraceable You") and requested her for the project; as with her other Paramount features, Rogers toiled during her off-hours at the studio's Long Island compound. She still swelled a minuscule role, that of the addle-brained companion of inebriated reporter Charlie Ruggles, but the picture itself was adult, handsome, well-acted and intelligently scripted, thus a distinct spotlight for her upwardly-mobile career. The narrative concerned a prosperous and free-thinking businessman (Fredric March) whose nonchalant advances frighten his secretary (Claudette Colbert) into marriage with a scoundrel (Monroe Owsley). After assorted intoxications, accidental shootings, and a brush with the law, the typist

FOLLOW THE LEADER (1930). With Ed Wynn

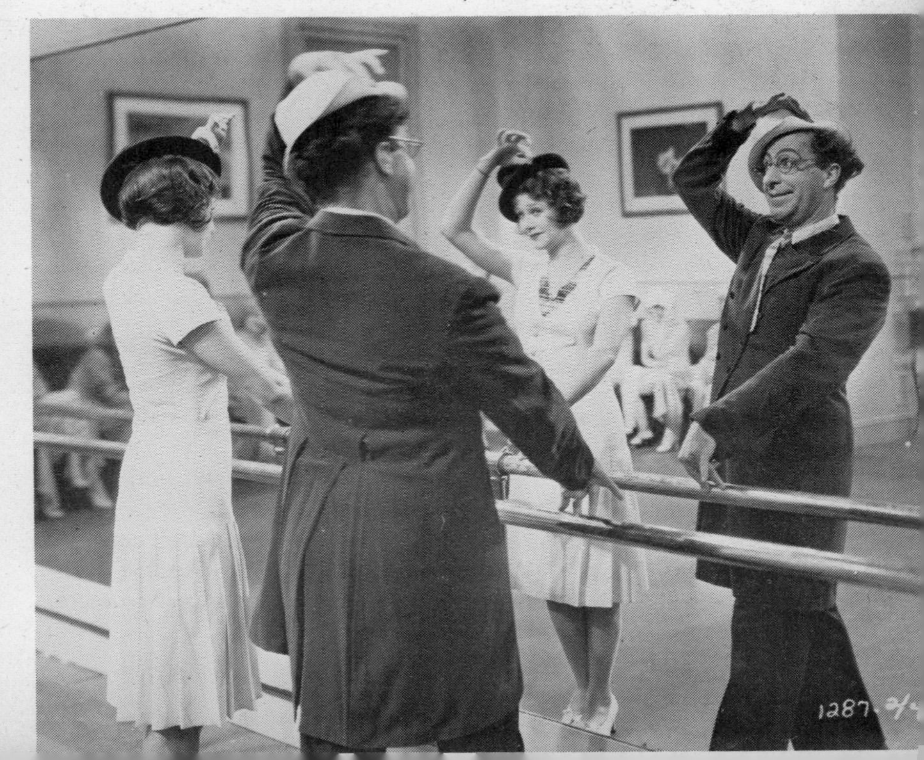

and her former boss disregard society's possible rebuke, abandon the worthless husband, and set sail for southern France together, a truly bold finale for the times. As the embroiled triangle, Colbert, March, and Owsley were prime.

Scarcely box-office bonanzas, Rogers' five Paramount features offered scant opportunity for creative development as well. That she was generally tagged as "bright," "lovely," or "attractive" by critics of the day was evidence not only of their blindness to her budding comedic talent, but also of the prettified nature of her Paramount appearances. So, in 1931, longing for better, she signed a contract, with RKO-Pathé and, Lela in tow whisked away to Hollywood.*

There, for the studio which was to later occupy her for nearly a decade, she co-starred in her first West Coast release, *The Tip Off,* directed by Albert Rogell, a tidy, low-key programmer with some unfettered bright moments. Eddie Quillan (a dated but ebullient performer) plays a radio repairman who mistakenly becomes entangled in an underworld vendetta; his only

*Hollywood legend insists that Paramount mogul Jesse Lasky released the actress with the prescient remark, "I'm afraid a day will come when I'll regret this!"

HONOR AMONG LOVERS (1931). With Charles Ruggles

THE TIP OFF (1931).
With Eddie Quillan

allies are Kayo McClure (Robert Armstrong), a boxing contender of dim faculties, and Kayo's dame, Baby Face (Rogers). She excels in her brief comic showcase: flouncy and winsome, as the befriender of Quillan and the guardian of Armstrong. Physically, she resembles Joan Blondell, with a flip, curly blonde hair-do; her voice is chirrupy, giggly, alternately tough and girlish. "A girl of my refinement," she announces in a petulant voice, "don't mix with a bruiser!" She has one reflective, heartfelt moment at the climax when, gun in hand, Kayo rushes away to defend Quillan. "If you go this time," she tells him, "I'm through with ya." A close-up reveals tears streaming down her face, make-up flowing. It is a gentle moment and Armstrong kisses her, slaps her affectionately and then departs. Naturally, all ends well for the trio. Unmomentous but agreeable—marred by flat visuals and often-cumbersome camera movements—*The Tip Off* boasts a vigorous comic portrayal by Armstrong, and Rogers' most ingenious role to date.

Two further movies helmed by Albert Rogell for Pathé followed: *Suicide Fleet* in 1931 and *Carnival Boat* in 1932. Rogers was squandered in the former as the darling of a trio of seamen, played by William Boyd (her real true love), Robert Armstrong, and James Gleason. When war erupts, the three become embroiled in a tepid and tedious plot pitting German U-boats against a disguised U.S. schooner, with plenty of old-fashioned flag-waving at the climax. Rogers was truly a frill in the story, and beau Boyd was a drab romeo besides. Only a single half-memorable joke: She signals I L-O-V-E Y-O-U from the Brooklyn Navy Yard to the ocean-bound destroyer, and the entire crew is enraptured by the message.

Boyd, later the screen's "Hopalong Cassidy," also figures in *Carnival Boat,* though somewhat more sincerely. The movie itself is a flimsy, cliché-ridden outing with Rogers cast as a sweet, innocent, subservient "carnival gal" who surrenders her livelihood, inexplicably, for marriage to a humdrum lumberjack. Only one scene actually occurs on the titular vessel, that being the occasion for Rogers to croon, "How I Could Go for You." Dressed, of course, in a virginal-white, ruffled dress at her entrance, she becomes the point of contention between son Boyd and father Hobart Bosworth. Father, who would like to bequeath his bustling lumber business to his scion, predictably sniffs at a carny woman. But Rogers has a brief flash of spirit, directed at disapproving dad, which sounded the informal keynote for her entire workaday career in films: "Just because we work for a living doesn't mean

SUICIDE FLEET (1931). With James Gleason and Robert Armstrong

CARNIVAL BOAT (1932). With William Boyd

THE TENDERFOOT (1932). With Joe E. Brown and Vivian Oakland

we're worse than anyone else!" Yet her part was tiny and the film was dreary, a forgettable slice of pablum about life and love in the brawling north woods, enlivened only by its episode of a runaway train with faulty brakes.

After *Carnival Boat,* her option with Pathé was dropped, and the budding starlet began a free-lance interval, contracting first with First National for *The Tenderfoot,* directed by Ray Enright in 1932.*

**The Tenderfoot* was one of four versions of George S. Kaufman's play, *The Butter and Egg Man*. Others were filmed in 1928, 1940, and 1953, only the first under its original title.

The lesser of her two teamings with the wide-mouthed comic, Joe E. Brown, it was a belabored farce with inferior production values and a middling, long-spun narrative. Brown, according to the yarn, is a Texas cowpuncher who becomes the "angel" for a Broadway-bound musical entitled *Her Golden Sin*. He goes starry-eyed over a stenographer, played by Rogers, who is angled into the property's leading role. When finances go awry, the costumes are confiscated prior to opening night; but the ensemble substitutes a set of Shakespearean garb (in which they perform contemporary melodrama), prompting the critics to wildly applaud the satire. Then a gaggle of racketeers enters the story line, inducing elaborate high jinks, makeshift perils, and a climactic shoot out before the inevitable "happy ending." Regrettably, Rogers is merely ornamental in the proceedings, and Brown, he of the melon mouth and obnoxious catcall, likewise flounders in an excruciating premise.

The Thirteenth Guest, directed by Albert Ray for Monogram in 1932, was an improvement, albeit humble. Based on a novel by Armitage Trail, the low-budget, mildly chilling mystery was hailed by *Variety* as "one of the best independent mystery features of the new year . . . vastly superior to many of the mystery themes produced by major companies during the past two years." Rarely seen today, *The Thirteenth Guest* (not to be confused with *The Mystery of the 13th Guest,* its 1943 remake) adheres to a time-worn familiarity in its intricate plot which centers on an eerie mansion, a baffling will, and strange killings by electrocution. Among the uniformly competent cast: Lyle Talbot impersonated a

THE THIRTEENTH GUEST (1932). With J. Farrell MacDonald (pointing) and Lyle Talbot (at right)

gumshoe who doggedly, and convincingly, pursued the clues; J. Farrell MacDonald, staunch as usual, played the local constabulary; and Brandon Hurst was humorously dull-witted as his sidekick. Of Rogers, whose role was tiny but impressive, it is sufficient to mention that she is the title caller: an heiress who nearly breathes her last.

Rogers is not, however, the title player of *Hat Check Girl,* her next release for Fox in 1932, although she does portray a hat check girl nonetheless, besides engaging in some genial bootlegging on the side. She is merely the pal of Sally Eilers, a nitery girl who becomes enmeshed in romance with a young playboy. A scandal-mongering columnist enters the fiction and departs with a well-aimed bullet in his lifeless body, causing the expected legal snags. Safe and efficient performances all around, from Eilers, Ben Lyon (as the playboy) and Monroe Owsley (as the cad), produced temperate if unspectacular fare. And Rogers, already pegged as a wise-cracking woman, with a vim, verve, and wit that were becoming recognizable, contributed another trustworthy performance in a secondary role. She had already begun to emanate an unaffected air, an ease and growing professionalism, that attracted favorable notice.

You Said A Mouthful, her last release in busy 1932, is one of Joe E. Brown's best (loosely speaking) comedies, no doubt due to the lean, economical direction of Warners' faithful Lloyd Bacon. With uncharacteristic finesse, Brown played the inventor of a "non-sinkable" bathing suit who goes westward to Los Angeles, thinking he is owed an inheritance; after a succession of mix-ups, he finds himself mistaken for a champion swimmer. There is, as expected, a Big Race, a marathon swim from Catalina Island; and, though Brown is a foresworn landlubber (he can't swim), he pits his "unsinkable" suit against Guinn Williams in the water match. Nothing is revealed by the disclosure that Brown wins handily, nor that the comedian is thankfully more subdued than usual in this so-so vehicle. As a vivacious flapper, Ginger manages to interject a few delicious moments of comic romance.

Warners director Mervyn LeRoy was dating Ginger steadily during these early days and, so the story goes, he urged her to accept a role as replacement for Joan Blondell in a movie titled *42nd Street.* It was fortunate advice, by any measure, for *42nd Street* was a top box-office hit of 1933; and, though sixth-billed, she was awarded her snappiest part to date in the character of chorine "Anytime Annie." The movie itself, as every buff knows, is one of the most exhilarating

A publicity pose for Twentieth Century-Fox

HAT CHECK GIRL (1932). With Sally Eilers and Monroe Owsley

backstage musicals of the Depression era, fraught with humor, sentiment, spectacle, and meaning. Lloyd Bacon directed in a breezy, ingratiating style, and Busby Berkeley, the inimitable maestro of kaleidoscopic tableaux, fashioned the elaborate musical numbers: "You're Getting To Be a Habit With Me," "I'm Young and Healthy," "Shuffle Off to Buffalo," and "Forty-Second Street."

A trend-setter and a sparkling original, *42nd Street* focuses on the predicament of stage director Warner Baxter, a hard-driving but sympathetic fellow who invests his failing health into one last property, a show called *Pretty Lady,* which teeters near collapse when the leading lady (Bebe Daniels) fractures her ankle on the eve before the opening. But the show must go on and Ruby Keeler, that dear, sweet tap-dancer, is enlisted from the ranks of the chorus to click her heels to glory. "You're going out a youngster," Baxter warns her desperately before the fateful curtain, "but you've got to come back a star!" She does, of course, and that bittersweet conclusion is only one of the reasons why *42nd Street* is, even today, roistering entertainment.

The musical owed its phenomenal popularity at the time, plus its lasting acclaim, to several striking currents beyond the utterly hypnotic Busby Berkeley groupings, the tour-de-force acting by the Warner Brothers stock company, and the blistering thrust of the story. For the trapped, impoverished folks of the Depression era, *42nd Street* was a grand, inflated parable of the foundering of capitalism and its piecemeal efforts to survive. The movie offered a celebration of individual initiative (Ruby Keeler, succeeding as only virtue must), community cooperation in the symbolic form of "rehearsals" ("You're going to dance your feet off," barks Baxter. "It's going to be the toughest six weeks you ever lived through!"), and an ethic of dynamic leadership (Warner Baxter, who prefigures FDR himself). These elements, in a plot line laden with references to breadlines, produced a greasepaint musical that was simultaneously "escapist" and relevant. And, nicely bolstering publicity, a lavish promotional train loaded with

42nd STREET (1933). In the chorus line with (at her left) Ruby Keeler and Una Merkel

42nd STREET (1933). With George E. Stone and Una Merkel

Warner Brothers stars (Rogers was aboard) trekked cross-country to salute Roosevelt's inauguration, dispensing ballyhoo (and expensive irony) at every whistle stop.

Rogers contributed mightily to the collaborative success: Her "Anytime Annie"—of whom it is remarked, "She only said no once and then she didn't hear the question"—is a little gem of characterization. She enters the saga during auditions for the *Pretty Lady* kick line, arriving pretentiously in a hired car, toting a pedigreed dog named Fifi, and displaying a monocle, a cane, and a hoity-toity accent. Her guise is immediately funny, as are her choice quips to the competition. Then she vanishes, becoming simply one of the many harried chorines of the show-within-the-show, surfacing momentarily in one song number, "Shuffle Off to Buffalo," with Una Merkel. But her most affecting moment occurs when, scorning her own chances, she pleads with Baxter to give "Sawyer" a.k.a. Ruby Keeler, an opportunity to play the lead.

"Listen," she entreats, a fragile edge in her voice, "I've been waiting years for a chance like this and, if I give it up, the kid must be good!" Rogers is persuasive and Ruby is catapulted to stardom. But, ironically, in real life, it was the bobbed blonde who captured the public fancy, and Ruby Keeler who departed from the scene after her brief popularity in the thirties.

Her next release, *Broadway Bad*, was unmistakably a backslide in quality. Directed for Fox by Sidney Lanfield, also the taskmaster of *Hat Check Girl*, this go-round sighted Rogers as a soft-hearted Broadway chorus girl (already ringing familiar) who is the loyal crony of Joan Blondell, also a showgirl, whose name becomes a lurid marquee draw when her wealthy, drink-sodden husband divorces her. Much of the plot was involved with legal wrangling over the couple's child. Though Blondell, one of the era's most reliable players, was believable (she resembled, physically and in type, Rogers herself) in her thankless role, and Ricardo Cortez was properly sleazy as the estranged husband, the story was

BROADWAY BAD (1933). With Joan Blondell

hopelessly middling. Rogers' role was merely gratuitous.

When Warren Beatty, in Arthur Penn's *Bonnie and Clyde,* ventures into a movie house for a celluloid respite, the sequence he views is of Ginger Rogers singing "We're in the Money" from *Gold Diggers of 1933*—an homage, thirty-five years later, to the pithy, opening sally of Mervyn LeRoy's follow-up (one of many) to *42nd Street*. Less trenchant and less sensational, *Gold Diggers of 1933* was nevertheless buoyed by a glittering cast which included Warren William, Joan Blondell, Aline MacMahon, Ruby Keeler, Dick Powell, Guy Kibbee, and Ned Sparks. It was the plot line which was hokey: the tale of a Boston blueblood (Dick Powell) who invests his money and self-penned tunes into a Broadway musical, only to be denounced by his high-minded brother (Warren William). The usual romantic cross-ups develop from this glib proposition. Busby Berkeley once again discharged extravaganza duty, with such memorable numbers as "Shadow Waltz," "Pettin' in the Park" and "I've Got to Sing a Torch Song". The final routine, "Remember My Forgotten Man,"

GOLD DIGGERS OF 1933 (1933). With Aline MacMahon, Ruby Keeler, and Joan Blondell

GOLD DIGGERS OF 1933 (1933). Singing "We're in the Money"

is perhaps the most outstanding of all Depression verses (the title was suggested by FDR's promise of a New Deal for the "forgotten man at the bottom of the economic pyramid") and surely the quintessential one. Sung by Joan Blondell (and reprised by black songstress Etta Moten), the number unwound elaborately against a backdrop of ex-GI's, a weary, hungry, ragged and despairing army.

Rogers' ornate solo introduced this movie as, saddled with the name of Fay Fortune, she sang "We're in the Money" in Pig Latin, while decked in a gaudy gown of coins, backed by a chorus of oscillating jumbo coins. (She insists that the idea for vocalizing in Pig Latin was hers; Darryl F. Zanuck, she claims, espied her frolicking on the set and decided to include the bit.) Even today, her introductory words ("We're in the money/We're in the money/We've got a lot of what/It takes to get along") echo wryly into the infinity of cinema myth, with an irony entirely in keeping with Rogers' insouciant and street-wise reputation. She was actually spotlighted in another number, a parody of Helen Morgan, performed in a black décolleté outfit at a chalk-white piano, which was cut from the released print. But she was merely the bottom-line member of the starving quartet of gold diggers —with little to do but wisecrack intermittently. However, the film's enormous success helped to launch her into her first starring role in a movie.

The movie, produced by RKO during her studio-hopping and directed by William A. Seiter, has few devotees nowadays. But *Professional Sweetheart,* a low-budget radio satire of the type which proliferated in Hollywood during the thirties, is a bristling, delectable comedy, albeit in a decidedly minor league, that finally showcased Rogers' comedic gifts and confirmed, for moviegoers and studio wags alike, that she had, indeed, the makings of a star. The delirious story was the precursor of later "screwball" comedies: Glory Eden (Rogers), the Purity Girl of the Ippsie-Wipsie Radio Hour, is bored with being the country's sweetheart and would prefer to smoke, drink, flirt with a few bounders, go to the devil (wherever he may be), and dance the sinful night away in Harlem. To mollify her, the sponsor selects a devoted fan by lottery to become her "fiancé." Wonder of wonders, she goes light-headed over the chosen yokel, and returns suddenly with him to his native Kentucky and, presumably, domestic bliss. Rival agents scramble to lure Glory back to the mike, a task which is accomplished, finally, by an agreement between the sponsor and his main competitor to institute the

PROFESSIONAL SWEETHEART (1933) With Theresa Harris

A SHRIEK IN THE NIGHT (1933). With Purnell Pratt

Ippsie-Kelsie Clothies Hour. One of Hollywood's choice backup casts, including Gregory Ratoff, Frank McHugh, Allen Jenkins, ZaSu Pitts, and Edgar Kennedy, invest this comedy with madhouse fever.

But it was Rogers, in her initial starring role, who showed a fetching presence and expert timing. In heavy make-up, especially lipstick, she is alternately petulant (refusing to autograph her contract until supplied with black-lace underwear) and supplicating in her masquerade as Glory Eden. "I want to sin and suffer and nobody will let me suffer!," she complains tearfully at one point. She is wed at midway on national hook-up (shades of Tiny Tim) and, at that juncture, the movie slackens and so does her implausibly domesticated personality. Before the enfeebling process, which happens to a movie that, frankly, is only quick-paced and amusingly unpretentious at best, she tosses a gleam of her future exuberance into this early vehicle. One curious note: RKO, wary of Rogers' pleasant if unremarkable voice, hired Etta Moten, who had appeared briefly in *Gold Diggers of 1933*, to dub her singing chores.

The actress then re-teamed with director Albert Ray and low-budget star Lyle Talbot for *A Shriek in the Night*, produced for Allied Pictures in 1933, a lively if derivative entry with one of lotus-land's favorite scenarios. She and Talbot, both first-rate and complementary, impersonated rival news-hounds who unravel the clues of a mystifying

DON'T BET ON LOVE (1933). With Lew Ayres

series of killings in a modern apartment house. In the course of the investigation, which ends satisfactorily just as Rogers is about to be stuffed into the house incinerator by the lunatic assassin, the two reporters also divine their affection for each other. Also in the cast was Purnell Pratt as the confounded police inspector, and the recurring Arthur Hoyt as his lamebrained subordinate.

Don't Bet On Love, directed by Murray Roth for Universal in 1933, collected fewer kudos. The lukewarm romantic trifle is interesting mainly in retrospect for the coupling of Rogers with future husband Lew Ayres, whose career had foundered badly since his prestigious role in Lewis Milestone's *All Quiet on the Western Front.* Mild-mannered Ayres, according to the scenario, was a luck-blessed plumber whose penchant for gambling (he picks twenty-six successive winners at Belmont) vexes his fiancée Rogers. She, a manicurist by trade, refuses to abide the fellow until his nasty habit is cured; needless to say, he ultimately loses in a big way, learns his lesson, and wedding bells chime. Roth also scripted, and the result is an actionless, ho-hum sketch with a surfeit of race-track shots and two stalwart players mired in the heap. But Rogers, at least, was elevated to an equal status in billing—a station she would rarely yield in the future—for her share in this elementary comedy.

The frivolous but entertaining *Sitting Pretty,* also released in 1933, was one of Paramount's seemingly endless string of frothy musicals. Speedily directed by Harry Joe Brown, and scored by Mack Gordon and Harry Revel (who appear in cameo as a music publisher and his partner), *Sitting Pretty* owes its spotty virtues to a trio of energetic leads: Jack Haley, Jack Oakie, and Ginger. Haley and Oakie played songwriters (among their titles, "Good Morning, Glory!") who hitchhike to Hollywood, encountering en route a lunatic who presents them with a bogus check for $100 as payment for a ditty, and also some Hollywood types, scarcely less insane, who establish them in the movies. Rogers, incidentally, is the sweet-tempered lunch-counter miss who tags along and stands fast at every possible emergency. One of the film's tunes, "Did You Ever See a Dream Walking?," enjoyed a nationwide popularity, but the movie itself, ingratiating though superficial, was not a tremendous hit. A battery of outlandish players spoofed the movie colony: Gregory Ratoff as a Hollywood agent; Lew Cody as a picture producer; and Thelma Todd as the femme luminary of Acme Studio, Rogers' rival for the attentions of Oakie.

In roughly three years, the young

SITTING PRETTY (1933). With Jack Oakie and Jack Haley

actress had tolled nineteen films, few outstanding and mostly box-office fodder of little lasting import. It was rather a grating indenture—of the type which Hollywood foisted with irritating regularity upon its ingénues, coercing them into weak-kneed testimonials against their own best interests or busying them as atmospheric ciphers—but there were compensations. She learned speed, not only in the film-making but in the composition of her character; henceforth she would be a no-nonsense actress of precision and dispatch. She learned variety too, in the tone of her pictures (establishing, for example, a persona that functioned creditably in either an urban or rustic context) and in the corollary style of her performance. And, finally, she acquired a security in manner that not only recommended her to a growing brood of fans and critics but also, in 1933, to RKO for a long-term contract.

She had reportedly tested at Columbia Pictures for studio boss Harry Cohn but Cohn, who had been intrigued by her early pictures, could not decide whether or not to sign the relative unknown. Merian C. Cooper, the eminent producer of films such as *King Kong* and *Little Women* (and, later, of many John Ford films), had supervised the shooting of *Professional Sweetheart,* and he too was intrigued. Cooper inspected the Columbia screen test—which, according to legend, was an "embarrassingly stilted" impersonation of a woman lawyer—and promptly signed Rogers to the standard seven-year deal with the studio. She was then forced to drop her scheduled role in Paramount's *Take A Chance* where she was replaced by June Knight. Cooper was planning a musical entitled *Flying Down to Rio* in which he intended to cast Dorothy Jordan, until their marriage revised his thinking. So, as these things happen, Ginger Rogers was teamed instead with a stage hoofer named Fred Astaire.

MAINLY ASTAIRE

But once more under the RKO logo, a pre-Astaire solo: *Chance at Heaven,* directed by William A. Seiter, was actually shot before *Flying Down to Rio* and released shortly afterward. A movie, in the piquant phrase of *Variety,* "in which nearly nothing happens," *Chance at Heaven* stars Joel McCrea and Marion Nixon (besides Rogers) in a rippling, love-triad melodrama concerning a bumpkin-like gas-station attendant (McCrea) who must choose a wife between socialite Nixon and loyal, small-townish Rogers. He opts for the former, an emancipated high-brow, but has cause to regret his decision. His bride becomes pregnant and, unwilling to be restricted by youthful motherhood, she flees to New York City where (it is strongly and surprisingly hinted) she secures an abortion. Of course, Rogers, who is tagged as the smart, sensible, maternal type of gal, is waiting around patiently to snag McCrea into a good, old-fashioned marriage at the finis. Sudsy but pleasant, with class-conscious and feminist overtones, *Chance at Heaven* is a late-night, drowsy sort of movie with few blemishes, even less dynamism.

Flying Down to Rio, meanwhile, released by RKO in 1933, directed by Thornton Freeland, is a milestone which, as an entity, may be considered a millstone. "It's an Astaire-Rogers movie only in the sense that the two of them are in it," writes Arlene Croce, whose *The Fred Astaire & Ginger Rogers Book* is the definitive profile of their teamwork. She adds, "It really belongs to prehistory along with *Dancing Lady* (Astaire's debut film) and the twenty-odd films that Ginger Rogers made before it."* The plot unceremoniously circumvents both stars (because, of course, they were not yet stars) to spotlight Gene Raymond, a band-leader who is enticed to Rio de Janeiro by Dolores Del Rio, a South American beauty, for the opening of a new hotel there by her father. Rogers and Astaire, fourth- and fifth-billed respectively, play tagalongs without any interrelationship. Rogers—thin, with a frizzy, fluffy blonde hair-do—sings "Music Makes Me" in her piping voice at the spirited opening, but Astaire is idle until the famed "Carioca" sequence at midway. He is sharing a table with Rogers in one of the typically posh night-spots of the period when the music begins to play. Couples begin to dance grotesquely to the Latin-esque rhythms, while there are cut-

*Arlene Croce, *The Fred Astaire & Ginger Rogers Book*, Outerbridge & Lazard, New York, 1972, p. 24.

aways to side bits of comic business. "I'd like to try this thing once," suggests Astaire, and on that cue, the couple stand, amble to the dance floor and proceed to steal the movie. Their forehead-to-forehead "Carioca"—too brief but flashy—made a distinct impression with audiences, with critics, and with RKO. Flimsy, slow-moving, and spiced by the studio's big-budget design—especially a gaudy, wing-walking spectacle at the climax that joined chorines and air-planes in the same kick line—the movie really only had two unquestionable nuggets: Astaire and Rogers. Their presence would make this musical, for decades hence, a revered "classic."

Yet it would be another year before their tandem éclat would be exploited. Rogers followed with a dud, *Rafter Romance,* also directed by the workaday Seiter, in 1934. Norman Foster co-starred as an impoverished night watchman who shares a Greenwich Village attic address with artist Rogers. They never meet—until a Sunday picnic—because one is a nightly tenant and the other resides by day. Also

CHANCE AT HEAVEN (1933). With Marion Nixon and Joel McCrea

FLYING DOWN TO RIO (1933). With Fred Astaire

RAFTER ROMANCE (1934). With George Sidney

in the cast is George Sidney as the landlord, and Robert Benchley, straining for laughs as the agent of an ice-box company. Even at seventy-two minutes, the movie was uninvolving, unfunny, and overlong.

Finishing School, which is heavily influenced by the German-made *Maedchen in Uniform,* deserves a small footnote in Hollywood history, at least, since it was co-scripted (with Laird Doyle) and co-directed (with George Nicholls, Jr.) by Wanda Tuchock. Tuchock, once an assistant to King Vidor, credited with the story on his *Hallelujah!,* only directed this one movie during her career. Interesting, if badly flawed, the movie offers a melodramatic view of an exclusive girls' boarding school, Crockett Hall, where the rules are more important than the students. Rogers, who played second lead to Frances Dee, is "Pony," the unofficial leader of the school chums, the prankster, the smart-aleck, the usual wiseacre; Dee, daughter of affluence, is the goody-goody type. But—in keeping with Rogers' crystallizing image—"Pony" turns out to be the virtuous child at heart, while Dee, in a weekend fling, must defend herself pathetically against the onslaught of her unprincipled escort. Among the eventual complications for Dee are an unwanted pregnancy, the contemplation of suicide, and a confrontation with her self-absorbed mother (Billie Burke); but the conclusion is happy and tidy, thanks to her chivalric boyfriend, hospital intern Bruce Cabot. Despite its mild statement against tradition and Rogers' generally comely role, *Finishing School* is standard Hollywood fare.

On loan-out, Rogers next sparked one of Warners' many interchangeable musicals, *20 Million Sweethearts*, directed by Ray Enright in 1934. It was a joke-laden radio satire, resembling *Professional Sweetheart*, with the actress again cast as the Cinderella dream-woman of a radio soap hour. Pat O'Brien, the top-liner, played an irrepressible, chatterbug radio agent who discovers Dick Powell, a singing waiter whose specialty number is "The Man on the Flying

FINISHING SCHOOL (1934). With Frances Dee

20 MILLION SWEETHEARTS (1934). *With Dick Powell*

Trapeze." It is true love between crooner Powell and songstress Rogers, but the airwaves sponsors (led by soap king Joseph Cawthorn, who declares that Powell lacks "soap appeal") strive to block their betrothal. Eventually, Powell scores a success with a Harry Warren-Al Dubin ditty entitled "I'll String Along With You," and all ends happily. Also in the cast: Allen Jenkins, a welcome stalwart on such occasions, has an amusing send-up as a kiddies' "Uncle Pete," a radio personality who takes his sandman role too seriously; and the quick-sighted may spot Leo F. Forbstein, Warners' ubiquitous conductor, in a cameo. Crackerjack performances from the entire cast, including Rogers, a chic, self-assured radio star who delivers one song at the outset, make for a bright, tuneful show in the run-of-the-mill backstage tradition of Warner Brothers.

John G. Blystone, whose career was mostly confined to shoestring budgets, directed the next Rogers outing, *Change of Heart,* for Fox in 1934. Based on the novel, *Manhattan Love Song* by Kathleen Norris, the movie brought together the team of Janet Gaynor and Charles Farrell, whose greatest success together was in the silent era, in movies such as Frank Borzage's *Seventh Heaven* in 1928. James

CHANGE OF HEART (1934). With James Dunn, Charles Farrell, and Janet Gaynor

Dunn and Rogers co-starred, with Gaynor and Farrell, as young college graduates who depart California to seek their fates and fortunes in teeming New York City. Once in Manhattan—an airplane travel sequence cross-country is handled nicely—their romantic proclivities are upended. Rogers played a reckless young lass, an heiress of small proportions, who pursues legal aide Farrell, though she really loves singer Dunn. (Watch for a very young Shirley Temple in the cast.) Well-done but ultimately cloying and dull, the movie is, in the terse words of *Variety*, "a nag that never quite gets started."

Ben Hecht's original story was revamped by Ben Markson for *Upper World* in 1934, directed by Roy Del Ruth for Warner Brothers. All parties involved are owed credit for the crisp urbanity of this suspense fable, a movie that is nicely contained within the small, capable scope of Del Ruth's vision. Warren William played Alexander Stream, a railroad magnate, whose wife (Mary Astor) neglects him for social affairs. Lonely and unhappy, he befriends a show girl (Rogers, still on loan-out), until a blackmailer (J. Carrol Naish) appears on the scene. The magnate soon finds himself innocently involved in a double murder. One of the corpses is Rogers herself, her only such demise in motion pictures; her death occurs when she valiantly stops a bullet intended for the bigwig. Such murky matters lead inevitably to a judicial inquiry, and the culmination is agreeable for everybody concerned but the long-gone Rogers. Sidney Toler gives a tangy performance as the traffic cop who is "broken" by the rich William after presenting him with a traffic summons, and then later doggedly tracks down the clues which lead to the real murderer. A savvy piece, *Upper World* prefigures—with its talk of the woebegone rich—the softer contours of *Fifth Avenue Girl* in 1940.

Then, in 1934, *The Gay Divorcee* arrived, and the American cinema was never quite the same again. Very few events in movie history can compare with the teaming of Astaire and Rogers. Their ten motion pictures, cherished by thousands of buffs today, were a rare triumph of style over content (a concept foreign to Hollywood). Busby Berkeley's musicals provide another instance of subordination to style, but Berkeley's special forte was mass spectacle while Astaire was the master of the solo dance. Or, with Ginger Rogers at his side, a twosome at most. The RKO production numbers—showy, elaborate, interminable, and patterned in black-and-white art deco—declined in importance as the series progressed, and the team's popularity rose.

In the Astaire-Rogers films the

UPPER WORLD (1934). With Warren William

THE GAY DIVORCEE (1934). With Edward Everett Horton

THE GAY DIVORCEE (1934). Dancing "The Continental" with Fred Astaire

dances were all, because the plots were overwhelmingly shallow, trivial, and recurrent: Boy meets girl, boy loses girl, boy gets girl, costarring Edward Everett Horton and Eric Blore, plus a complement of songs. These movies were escapist fun, yes—see how often Astaire allowed himself a self-consciously serious number, such as "Night and Day" or "They Can't Take That Away From Me" in comparison to the light routines—but they were also artistic and involving, in their finest moments, in a way that other Hollywood musicals never approached. Even Berkeley, whose genius was more decorative and abstract, never tugged the heart in the manner of an Astaire-Rogers dance. They were not only the highlights of their movies but, frequently, they were the *only* lights. Their movies have weathered the passage of time to transcend the simple evaluation of "good" or "bad" and to create their own class, Astaire-Rogers. That class was front-rank.

Directed by Mark Sandrich, a one-time physicist who was to direct five of the Astaire-Rogers vehicles, *The Gay Divorcee* introduces all the best, most amicable elements of the series. Astaire is Guy Holden, a musical-comedy hoofer, who is love-struck by Mimi Glossop (Rogers), an unhappily married woman in search of a divorce. When Mimi employs a professional gigolo (a florid Erik Rhodes who declares, "Whichever way the wind is blowing, that is the way I sail!") to provoke a correspondent suit, that is reason enough, in the minds of RKO scenarists, for nearly two hours of mix-up, catch-up, coupling, uncoupling, singing, dancing, and bedroom farce. Eric Blore has a few scenes as a waiter who becomes the plot's *deux ex machina*, but Edward Everett Horton, that supremely tonic personality, is simply magnificent as the perpetually bewildered aide-de-camp of Astaire; he pauses his run of double takes to croon "Let's K-nock K-nees" with a chubby Betty Grable, his only such singalong in the series.

Astaire is, as Astaire always is, the long-suffering ("Men don't pine, girls pine; men just suffer!") debonair romeo whose solo routine in the movie, "A Needle in a Haystack," is danced alone in his living room. He clicks his heels and

ROMANCE IN MANHATTAN (1934). With Sidney Toler, Francis Lederer, and J. Farrell MacDonald

whirls his props with an ease so light and an authority so unassuming that he leaps into the pantheon of screen heroes almost automatically. His presence was, like Chaplin's, ethereal, magical, otherworldly; he didn't abide by earthbound rules, and he imagined his own limitations. His essence was control, in style as well as in technique; the dances, of course, were devised by him and choreographer Hermes Pan. But he also supervised the camera movement, which he kept tight and natural on the dances themselves; the dropping of cutaway shots, which were used to leaven the monotony of the dance routines, was also his innovation. Such was his imagination, his intelligence, his creative wellspring, that he injected genius into some of the most abominable frameworks ever devised by Hollywood and, incredibly, made them work.

His dances with Rogers in *The Gay Divorcee*—"no more thrilling or more musical dance had ever been presented on the screen than Cole Porter's slow, seductive 'Night and Day'," in Arlene Croce's words—are sublime. But if he is already polished, in *The Gay Divorcee,* Rogers is not yet in her stride. The actress is limited in her part—the Astaire-Rogers films never called for full-blown characterizations—to fleeing his clutches and otherwise glowing intermittently. When they finally join forces, alas, it is the occasion for the climactic "The Continental," a near-record eighteen-minute ensemble dance which drones on endlessly.*

One of Rogers' most fetching showcases, independent of Astaire, was *Romance in Manhattan,* her next movie, directed by Stephen Roberts for RKO. It is a heartwarming romance about a Czech immigrant (played with ingratiating charm by Francis Lederer) who is rejected at the port of entry in New York City because he is unable to pay the entrance fee. He manages to slip through a porthole and swim ashore, where, hungry and penniless, he wanders the streets of the city. Luckily, he is befriended by a sweet-hearted chorine (Rogers). One of her most likable, quintessential roles, as a working-class showgirl who cares for her younger brother, newsboy Jimmy Butler, she is a slang-tossing, strong-willed, self-supporting woman with a jaundiced view of the globe. He tenants him-

*In March, 1934, Rogers' lawyers filed suit against station KFI, San Francisco's NBC affiliate, for broadcasting over the radio an interview with a person claiming to be "Ginger Rogers." The program's hostess, who gave advice to the stars, had received RKO's permission to have the radio impersonator confess that she, "Rogers," was more capable at musical comedy than dramatic roles. "Ginger Rogers" also admitted on the air that she should eat more Health Bread. The suit ended amicably, but it was the opening sally in the long battle between RKO and the real Ginger Rogers.

ROBERTA (1935). The Countess Scharwenka (nee Lizzie Gatz) sings "I'll Be Hard to Handle."

ROBERTA (1935). Dancing with Fred to "Smoke Gets in Your Eyes"

self on her roof and hawks newspapers for a livelihood, even, in one of the most reprehensible subplots in the RKO file, scabbing as a taxi driver during a bitter strike in order to earn the $200 necessary for his legal papers. When dire complications ensue and he is threatened with deportation, the big-hearted police of New York City hurry to the rescue, and citizenship, marriage, and myth are secured in one swift stroke.

Unobtrusively directed by Roberts, the movie is marred by its flag-waving, its neurotic emphasis on wealth (a montage of "America" at the beginning focuses on banks, surety buildings, and the overheard street talk of people discussing cash), its reactionary attitude toward labor, and Lederer's Pollyanna frame of mind toward America. These elements, however, are forgettable; and Rogers, characteristically aloof from the politics of the movie, is soft-hard, resilient, wistful and touching in one of her first roles of neither pasteboard nor type.

Jerome Kern's *Roberta* was next on the Astaire-Rogers slate in 1935, and Irene Dunne and Randolph Scott shared billing. One of their rarest pictures today, unavailable for television, *Roberta* is a jazzy, watchable movie that is important because it established Ginger Rogers as an equal in the partnership. The stage show, with a book by Otto Harbach, was reshaped by a host of RKO scenarists, including Allan Scott (RKO's workhorse), and the Kern score was likewise juggled, with songs like "Smoke Gets in Your Eyes" retained from the Broadway version, while several tunes by Dorothy Fields and Jimmy McHugh (in collaboration with Kern) were added. The plot was an outrageous potpourri: blending a burly American (Scott) with a fashion designer (Dunne) who is really a Russian princess, in Paris. Astaire and Rogers are helpmates, he as the bandleader of the Wabash Indianians, and she as the Countess Scharwenka, née Lizzie Gatz from Indiana. She is Astaire's old chum, who croons for a living at the Café Russe where "you have to have a title to croon." Love among the foursome goes unrequited until, in the Ziegfeld Follies tradition, the climactic musical fashion show. That is when the gawky Scott is finally united with luminous Irene Dunne; she, incidentally, sings three lilting songs: "Smoke Gets in Your Eyes," "Yesterdays," and "Lovely to Look At." William A. Seiter, directing in the absence of Sandrich, who was preparing *Top Hat,* was equally amicable, which is why the movie, though slack and frothy, is rather enjoyable.

Astaire and Rogers surmount the airiness of *Roberta* to emerge swimmingly. Their choice moment together occurs during a "spon-

STAR OF MIDNIGHT (1935). With William Powell, Robert Emmett O'Connor, and J. Farrell MacDonald

taneous" tap routine on the dance floor of the Café Russe. The number is "I'll Be Hard to Handle," performed for the café workers, a light, bouncy and vibrant give-and-take of the type they made their own. It was during this routine that Rogers, intoning in a husky accent, slipped in an unannounced imitation of Lyda Roberti (who played the stage part of Lizzie Gatz), singing in Roberti's famous scat-patter for hilarious results. Rogers and Astaire float merrily in and out of the indifferent plot, and are paired several times again, for "I Won't Dance" and its reprise that closes the film, and for a brief dance to "Smoke Gets in Your Eyes."

One of the better *Thin Man* imitations proliferating in Hollywood in the mid-thirties was RKO's entry, *Star of Midnight* in 1935, teaming Rogers with the suave William Powell (à la Nick and Nora Charles). Like *Romance in Manhattan,* it was directed by Stephen Roberts, who handled the byzantine mystery adroitly. The title is a double pun: The mysterious Mary Smith, an actress appearing on Broadway in a play entitled *Midnight,* vanishes one evening

TOP HAT (1935). Dancing "Cheek to Cheek"

after her performance; on the same night, a reporter from the *Star*, a tabloid newspaper, who is hot on the trail of a scoop concerning the star of *Midnight*, is killed in the drawing room of lawyer Clay Dalzell (Powell). Dalzell's solution—Mary Smith, the elusive star, is never actually on-camera —is not only intricately conceived but, in the witty, urbane tradition of Powell's sleuthing, executed with gentlemanly polish. Rogers is on hand as a perky heiress, quick with the quip, who assists the investigation while seeking to entrap lawyer Dalzell into marriage. The two stars fuse nicely, in a counterpoint of manners and connivance, and the entire undertaking is tossed off lightly as brisk, insignificant fun.

Top Hat, directed by Mark Sandrich in 1935, is, perhaps, the most famous and arguably the best of the Astaire-Rogers musicals. There are slavish echoes of *The Gay Divorcee* in the Dwight Taylor-Allan Scott scenario but the lines are smoother, and *Divorcee*'s hybrid musical mixture of Porter and Hollywood tunesmiths is supplanted by a superb Irving Berlin score. The story, as per usual, is slight: It opens with Astaire in London's elite Thackeray Club, where, after members get annoyed at his noisy folding of a newspaper, he drops a volley of taps on the threshold before departing. A dancer, he falls in love-at-first-sight with Dale Tremont (Rogers), but she mistakes him for his own theatrical agent, Horace Hardwick (Edward Everett Horton), who is married. The pursuit leads to RKO's grandiose conception of Venice, where, in the moonlight and aboard an adrift gondola, matters are romantically resolved.

Besides Horton, who is humorously cast as the bug-eyed suspect in extra-marital affairs, the movie boasts Helen Broderick as his wife, a cool, skeptical spouse who is bemused by her husband's supposed amorous adventures. Erik Rhodes is Beddini (mirroring his Tonetti of *The Gay Divorcee*), a puffed-up fashion designer, and Rogers' traveling companion, whose motto is, "For the women the kiss, for the men the sword." Trusty Eric Blore, he of the withering glance, who graced five Astaire-Rogers films, plays Horton's valet who hovers on the edges of the entire affair. With such a cast, *Top Hat* is the most integrated of the Astaire-Rogers musicals, delectable and gay, balanced equitably between comedy, romance, and music, while containing some of the most memorable musical sequences ever captured on film.

Each number, excepting the satirical and insignificant "Piccolino" which is buoyed both by Berlin's mocking lyrics and Rogers' singing, is beautifully effective. Astaire breaks into song in the mid-

TOP HAT (1935). Fred and Ginger

dle of a sentence in his "No Strings (I'm Fancy Free)," a terrific, cascading living-room tap dance that looses plaster upon the head of a sleeping Rogers below. That is the cause for harsh words—and their introduction—before a contrite and fully bewitched Astaire caresses her back to slumber with a soft-shoe sandman coda. Later, when he pursues her to a bandstand in a London park, their number together, "Isn't This a Lovely Day To Be Caught in the Rain?," is cued by thunder and lightning. They lunge into a challenge tap dance which is fresh, exciting, and ecstatic forty years after the making. Without cutaways, without props, with the moment to themselves, they render a love-making dance that is as seemingly natural and spontaneous as the surrounding weather. That moment is topped, or perhaps equaled, by Astaire alone in his classic "Top Hat, White Tie and Tails," an evening-dress routine with a male chorus that is indescribably elegant, ostensibly performed as a sequence in Astaire's stage show-within-the-show.

Finally, in Venice, the duo rejoin for "Cheek to Cheek," a lovely, dreamy, romantic adagio which consummates their fitful romance. She was the perfect sparring partner, the ultimate lover, bending and swaying to his pull, his guidance, his tempo. She was womanly to his manliness and in *Top Hat* their dancing teamwork reached a pitch that would rarely, if ever, be surpassed in its pulsating achievement, even by themselves.

By now, Ginger Rogers was no longer an unknown commodity,* and RKO was persuaded to star her singly in *In Person,* a musical with songs by Oscar Levant and Dorothy Fields, directed in 1935 by the redoubtable William A. Seiter. It was an abject failure, then, and still has little appeal today. Rogers played a screenland star who flees the autograph hounds by donning bizarre make-up (black wig, buck teeth) and absconding to a rustic mountain retreat, where George Brent, a strong-silent mountaineer, engages her passions. Hermes Pan, the Astaire-Rogers choreographer, dutifully provided the dancework for this curio. Rogers bravely ranged the musical gamut, dancing, in a homemaker's pinafore, alone in her kitchen, for "Got a New Lease on Life," and then moving sinuously, for the sirenish "Out of Sight, Out of Mind," among a passel of dinner-jacketed men. Though she was winsome and adept, she was simply overburdened by the preposterous material in Allan Scott's scenario. And, besides, she required a more flexible foil, someone like Astaire, rather than the stolid Brent, for such a high-strung musical.

Follow the Fleet, an Irving Berlin musical based (loosely) on a 1922 play called *Shore Leave,* was next in 1936. Directed again by Sandrich, with a resemblance to *Roberta,* its restricted rights prevent widespread movie-house revivals nowadays. The movie is nearly two squirming hours long, a length, it might be irreverently suggested, that could be forgivably trimmed by excising songstress Harriet Hilliard (later Ozzie Nelson's Harriet of television fame) and lumbering Randolph Scott from the print. The story involves romantic problems between two Navy gobs and their shore gals, incidentally sisters. The

*In the fall of 1935, Rogers protested her treatment by the studio by ensconcing herself in a mountain retreat and refusing to appear for shooting until her contract was revised. She demanded more money, equal billing and publicity (with Fred Astaire), and a $10,000 bonus. After RKO threatened to team Jessie Matthews with Astaire in *Follow the Fleet,* she signed a new contract with the studio for a hefty increase in salary.

IN PERSON (1935). With George Brent

usual artificial enmity between Rogers and Astaire is thankfully abolished at the outset by the news that they are an ex-vaudevillian dance team. When he proposed marriage, she refused, believing it would damage her hoofing career. So he sullenly set sail. Now, as the fleet sets anchor in San Francisco, he joyously discovers that his long-lost team-mate is a singer in a cheap dance hall, so all is immediately forgiven. Their principal dilemma is uniting Scott and Hilliard (who turned brunette for the movie, in deference to Rogers), and only RKO could lavish two hours on such an unsympathetic premise.

But the movie contains some of their most rapturous routines. Not only the sailor jigs—"We Saw the Sea" and "I'd Rather Lead a Band," which are Astaire's solo spots—but also their precise, soaring teamwork. The numbers include: "Let Yourself Go," explosively rendered by the team in a dance-hall contest; "I'm Putting All My Eggs in One Basket," their goofiest-ever routine, complete with miscues, mugging rivalry and heads comically bumped together; and "Let's Face the Music and Dance," aboard sister Hilliard's

FOLLOW THE FLEET (1936). As Sherry Martin

ship for the large-scale finale, an awesome, audacious, and sensuous story-dance that ices the movie with breathtaking finesse. Rogers also had a solo dance, one of only two in the Astaire-Rogers series (the other is in *The Story of Vernon and Irene Castle*), which happens as she auditions for a theatrical producer. It was a short routine, too short, but it showed that she was a cheeky and improved tap dancer whose nimble solo talent was never fully employed. By *Follow the Fleet,* the team's rapport, in dialogue as well as dance, was electric.

George Stevens, a craftsman who began his career as an underling on Laurel and Hardy features and later directed such disparate gems as *Woman of the Year* and *Shane,* fashioned *Swing Time* as the next Astaire-Rogers teaming in 1936. With *Top Hat,* it is the most enduring, most successful of their motion pictures, one of the handful of exquisite musical "classics" of genuine artistry. The story, which kidded *Top Hat* by having a well-dressed Astaire hop a freight, was trivial: Astaire and Rogers played a dance team kept apart by the sweetheart (Betty Furness) back home, an innocent hypothesis which led to complications and breathless musical chairs of matri-

FOLLOW THE FLEET (1936). Typical Fred-and-Ginger attitudes: he wistful, she wary

SWING TIME (1936). Dancing to "Pick Yourself Up"

SWING TIME (1936). With Helen Broderick, Victor Moore, and Fred Astaire

mony at the climax. But what mattered was the musical routines: "Pick Yourself Up," an exhilarating dance duet in bubbly tempo; "The Way You Look Tonight," a ballad sung by Astaire to a lather-haired Rogers, which won the Academy Award for 1936; "Waltz in Swing Time," a spine-tingling number which Arlene Croce calls "the most rapturously sustained, endlessly reseeable of all their dances"; "A Fine Romance," a lilting melody with gently mocking lyrics, sung by both in a snowy musical setting; "Bojangles of Harlem," Astaire's blackface routine, something possibly only an artist of his calibre could get away with, an homage to Bill "Bojangles" Robinson that utilizes trick photography, elaborate black-and-white tones, and off-rhythm dancing; and "Never Gonna Dance," the plaintive final dance which Croce calls not only "the end of the affair," but also "the end of Astaire and Rogers' Golden Age."

Jerome Kern's score was exquisite; the direction by Stevens, though poky, was (thanks to the graceful photography by David Abel) exceptionally fluid; and, among the cast, Victor Moore and Helen Broderick delivered sharp and funny support. Astaire and

Rogers were in an expansive mood, teasing the movie along with abundant security, charm, and panache. They were never better.*

How did the two stars devise their routines? Often, Astaire and Rogers labored for eight weeks previous to filming, perfecting numbers that their directors, including Sandrich, never actually saw before shooting began. Astaire and Hermes Pan, the Nashville-born choreographer of Greek ancestry, would scan the script, study the score and, in the words of Pan, "just fool around, just fool around for hours." They would experiment for one week, typically, before inviting Rogers around for the second week of rehearsal. Frequently, the actress would spend this week observing the two men as the dances assumed shape. Pan usually took her part during these early rehearsals—"I know how she dances and what she expects from

*During the filming of *Swing Time,* Rogers played the trump card which eventually released her from partnership with Astaire. She refused to appear for rehearsals until her contract was adjusted. By now, her bargaining power was considerable, and she was placed on a fifty-two-week basis instead of the customary forty-week basis, as per her wishes. And, importantly, she was limited by the terms of her new contract to four films yearly, two with Fred Astaire and two without.

SHALL WE DANCE (1937). Ginger and Fred in Central Park, wondering whether to "call the whole thing off."

Astaire," he once explained—and was known, for certain of their movies, to have dubbed the actual tap sounds on the sound track for her during post-production work at RKO. Sometimes, the two stars did their dancing twice. For the camera, they danced in plain-soled shoes without metal taps, negotiating the polished, gleaming studio floors. Then, when the negative was printed, they would enclose themselves in a soundproof recording room at the studio and tap their dances in synchronization.

After two weeks of preliminary rehearsal, two or three weeks of serious polishing began, to be followed by several weeks of day-long rehearsal. Feet were known to bleed and tempers were known to flare. Astaire was a grueling perfectionist, and Hermes Pan and director Sandrich were also considered politely sadistic. The preparation for their routines ruffled Rogers, no slouch but hardly a fanatic either, on more than one well-rumored occasion. Producer Pandro Berman once described their partnership as "six years of mutual aggression." So torturous, for example, was the shooting of the final sequence in *Swing Time,* that forty-seven takes were required. It has been said that at wrap-up the feet of both players were bleeding, she was wearing her fourth skirt and he had already ravaged his sixth evening shirt.

Even without the rehearsals, their dance sequences were marathons; often they would dance for eighteen hours before the camera for a concise four-minute sequence on the screen. It was something the audiences never realized, because the facade was taste, class, perfection—without perspiration. "Sandrich reportedly has a sadistic theory," *The New York Times* reported upon one occasion, "that the more tired she and Astaire are, the better they are likely to be; he spends hours just wearing them down, reducing the couple virtually to a state of automatism."*

Slave driver Sandrich also helmed *Shall We Dance,* next for Astaire-Rogers in 1937, a savory little trifle which again had the bonus advantage of Edward Everett Horton and Eric Blore, plus a wonderfully hummable score by George and Ira Gershwin. Astaire played "the great Petrov" in the throw-away story, whose love for musical-comedy star Rogers provokes headlines, a forced "marriage," and the usual flurry of confusions. Horton is manager of the classical dancer, Petrov (né Peters), while Blore is a hotel manager who goes slightly mad trying to understand the goings-on-and-off. The musical numbers, as usual, elevated the belabored story line: "I've Got

*A detailed portrait of their workaday life, from which much of this description is taken, can be found in the December 12, 1936, issue of *Literary Digest*.

SHALL WE DANCE (1937). "They All Laughed"

Beginner's Luck," an Astaire solo quickie; "Slap That Bass," an upbeat ditty set in a ship's engine room, with singalong by the workers; "They All Laughed," a song by Rogers which leads to a typically ebullient Astaire-Rogers duet; "Let's Call the Whole Thing Off," a delightful, original roller-skating debate set in a Central Park rotunda, a dance so fanciful that it must be seen to be properly relished; "They Can't Take That Away From Me," the Gershwin standard, sung by Astaire to Rogers aboard a ferry bound to New Jersey where, according to the topsy-turvy plot, they can be married, then divorced (abbreviated in *Shall We Dance*, the song was reprised, thankfully, ten years later for their *The Barkleys of Broadway*); finally, "Shall We Dance," the obligatory spectacle. The last-named number cleverly had Astaire dancing with a chorus of soubrettes with face masks of Ginger Rogers (thereby salving his conscience for the misdeeds of the story) until she herself appears in the line-up.

It was a wily stroke to cast Astaire as the aesthete and Rogers as his commercial counterpart, since it allowed believably for their mild antagonisms, their differing styles, and the raison d'être of one of their most vibrant, if uneven,

STAGE DOOR (1938). With Ann Miller, Eve Arden, and Lucille Ball

vehicles. Rogers was in her stride, endearing, supple, composed, and it was a pity to see her function, in the loose-knit *Shall We Dance,* as merely the formula sweetheart out of RKO's hard-pressed idea bank. The presence of Harriet Hoctor, who dances "They Can't Take That Away From Me" with Astaire in Rogers' stead, merely aggravates the misery.

One of the zingiest comedies of the thirties was Gregory La Cava's masterly *Stage Door,* for which he copped the New York Film Critics prize for best direction in 1937. Breezy and tart, affecting as well as amusing, the movie is a pre-feminist feminist comedy that mocks, embarrasses and betters the then-current Hollywood crop of so-called "women's" pictures. Not only did La Cava unleash a puissant Rogers, fresh and confident from her Astaire triumphs, but it was also a heavenly conjunction of talent from RKO's ensemble of women. Among the cast were Gail Patrick, Constance Collier, Andrea Leeds, Lucille Ball, Eve Arden, Ann Miller and, representing the men, Grady Sutton, Jack Carson and Adolphe Menjou as an unscrupulous, lecherous producer. Katharine Hepburn, Rogers's rival on the RKO lot, co-starred (as the patrician) with Rogers (as the plebeian) in the lives, loves, and hard times of would-be actresses in a theatrical boarding-house.

The events center on a blueblood (Hepburn) with marquee ambitions; a starving, self-denying thespian (Leeds) with single-minded ambition to play the one role which eludes her; and a street-wary hoofer (Rogers), whose cynicism lands her on the casting couch. Rogers established her comedic skill with a force and intelligence that few of her later directors would ever adequately explore. She is the shepherd of the flock at the Footlights Club, the one with the kind word or the fast quip, depending on the occasion. When the cold, aloof, high-minded Hepburn moves her mountainous belongings in with Rogers, she cracks, "We could leave the trunks here and sleep in the hall . . . no use crowding the trunks." Hepburn sizes her up aptly: "You bark a lot but you don't bite." Her resolve is melted, naturally, and they become buddies.

When a suicide—the melodramatic demise of Andrea Leeds, distraught over losing her long-sought role to Hepburn—ruptures the complacency of life at the Footlights Club, Rogers shines through tearfully with an unsullied sincerity that carries the moment. It was a gorgeous performance that showed what Astaire overshadowed and what the future, in theory, augured. La Cava's masterwork has a gallery of similarly superb performances, fine

STAGE DOOR (1938). With Katharine Hepburn

camerawork by Robert De Grasse, a tight, witty scenario by Morrie Ryskind and Anthony Veiller (who dusted off the Edna Ferber-George S. Kaufman play, embellishing Rogers' part) and stylish direction that make for one of Hollywood's most humanly enjoyable comedies.

Having Wonderful Time, directed by Alfred Santell for RKO in 1938, was based on a popular play by Arthur Kober (who also scripted) about a summer camp in the Catskills. The Broadway play was riddled with plenty of ethnic jokes and a persistent thread of observation about the nine-to-five life of a young secretary who escapes the metropolitan pressures for a vacation at the camp. Producer Pandro S. Berman, RKO's ubiquitous overseer whose name adorns most of Rogers' RKO output, decided, perhaps on the basis of his gentile star, to switch the locale of the story to a more cosmopolitan setting. The Jewish in-jokes were dropped, and so were the observations of white-collar life. Contemporary opinion is unanimous that the play was superior but, for those today who lack the comparison, the movie has its gentle (if admittedly minor) allure. Rogers is the runaway to Camp Kare-Free, a retreat where the mosquitoes compete for attention with love-crazed waiters, moonlight romeos, and college graduates. Here she meets and is wooed by Douglas Fairbanks, Jr., and both deliver amenable if unremarkable performances. Fluffy and light-hearted, with the slick look of a solid programmer, *Having Wonderful Time* is bolstered by the RKO stock company of Lucille Ball, Eve Arden, Donald Meek, Ann Miller, Jack Carson, Grady Sutton, and even Red Skelton. Rogers coasts through the exercise with the self-amused style of a conspirator.

How promising it must have seemed in concept: a romance between Jimmy Stewart, an appealing, gangling young actor with a brace of minor credits, as a botany professor; with Ginger Rogers, herself on the threshold of dizzying solo stardom, as a nightclub hoofer. Director Howard Hawks was to draw on essentially the same idea three years later, with Barbara Stanwyck and Gary Cooper, two corollary stars, and evolve an unsung classic with *Ball of Fire*. Yet the difference between Hawks' lean, crackling comedy and the bumbling *Vivacious Lady*, directed by George Stevens, is the distance between raw idea and polished conception. *Vivacious Lady* has its avid partisans, but it is a movie that never quite clicks on its kinetic foundations.

The yarn: When an ill-at-ease

HAVING WONDERFUL TIME (1938). With Douglas Fairbanks, Jr.

VIVACIOUS LADY (1938). With James Stewart and Charles Coburn

Stewart visits a New York City night club to retrieve his cousin (James Ellison), he goes suddenly misty-eyed over a splashy dancer named Francey (Rogers). They embark on a night-long excursion in the metropolis, one of the most enthralling, schmaltzy sequences in an otherwise slapstick movie; they eat corn-on-the-cob, bare their souls, and brag until dawn. Then, before the first reel ends, they marry, a fatal scripting error, and (after spending their honeymoon in separate quarters on a crowded train) they arrive in Old Sharon, or what is ostensibly Collegetown U.S.A. Daddy Charles Coburn, president of the college, is on hand to greet them, unaware of the marriage; Stewart, fearing father's wrath at his "scandalous" marriage to a chorine, introduces Francey as his cousin's girlfriend. Thus, still without a honeymoon, the game but edgy girl becomes a botany student, Stewart plots to inform Coburn diplomatically, and the students of Old Sharon, especially Grady Sutton, ogle and whistle at their new, surprisingly mature classmate.

When Coburn's wife (Beulah Bondi), a woman who fakes a heart attack whenever her blustery husband enters a fit of rage, is discovered to be sympathetic to the young-marrieds, the farcical ending is trumpeted. Both women, mother-in-law and Rogers, angry and inconsolable, board a New York-bound locomotive and discover each other's presence in the midst of a crying contagion. Wiser and chastened, Coburn and Stewart manage to board the train and make amends. Francey and the professor are finally together as their compartment door slams and the last gag is cued: a whoo-whoo whistle from the speeding train.

Slowly paced, like many of Stevens' movies, but with many truly uproarious moments, the film has its greatest trouble stretching a solitary joke: that of Francey's unconsummated honeymoon with Professor Stewart. It was a perfectly repressed theme-symbol for that screen era, if not for the entire career of Ginger Rogers. But the actress, who quotes from the Astaire epics at one point by dancing the "Big Apple" with Beulah Bondi, never, alas, receives an opportunity to extend or improve the wistful vivacity of her first several minutes in the picture. She was not misused but, in fact, barely used.

Except for their initial venture, *Carefree,* directed by Mark Sandrich in 1938, was not only the weakest Astaire-Rogers vehicle but also (in eighty-three minutes) the shortest. Curiously, its saving grace was Ginger Rogers. In the words of Arlene Croce: "*Carefree* is more screwball comedy than musical, and it is more Ginger Rogers' film than Fred Astaire's." The script, patched together by no less than six RKO scenarists, featured Rogers as a radio songstress attached romantically to attorney Ralph Bellamy. Because she is indecisive about marriage, Bellamy recommends his analyst friend, Fred Astaire, whose equipment is mainly optical and whose assistant is burly Jack Carson. Her "complex maladjustment" is heightened by her contact with Astaire and the impending marriage with Bellamy self-destructs. During a drug-induced slow-motion dance, "I Used To Be Color-Blind," she instead asserts her love for the good doctor. Aghast at such treachery, Astaire hypnotizes her and administers an anesthetic which unchains her inhibitions. After a consultation with his own inner psyche, via a conversation with the mirror, Astaire decides that he has been too hasty in spurning her embrace. The chase is on, and, after a scramble, a marriage with Bellamy is averted at the last minute by Astaire.

Delirious in concept but soggy in execution, *Carefree* is also the least musical of their musicals. Besides "The Yam" and "Change Partners," the movie boasts only Astaire's high-stepping classic, "Since They Turned 'Loch Lomond' into Swing," a golf-course jaunt. As

CAREFREE (1938). An advertisement for the film

CAREFREE (1938). As Amanda

Arlene Croce writes: "It's Ginger Rogers who carries most of the 'spoof' material, and though she doesn't, in her scenes of mayhem, bring to it much more than a calculated cuteness (how mechanical, after all, was that late-Thirties tradition of lady stars kicking up their heels), she's oddly compelling in that double way of hers; she's like a clever puppy who knows it's being watched."*

The end, when it came, was honorable: *The Story of Vernon and Irene Castle* in 1939. What other saga could be so well suited to Astaire and Rogers than the musical biography of the dance team who, two decades earlier, had aroused similar national acclaim, the popularizers of the Bunny Hug, the Turkey Trot, and the Castle Walk? H. C. Potter, a leisurely director whose specialty was evocative period-pieces, beautifully conjured a turn-of-the-century atmosphere for RKO and, though truncated and low-key, the movie was a memorably dramatic coda for one of the screen's most singular series.

The roles of Vernon and Irene

**The Fred Astaire & Ginger Rogers Book*, p. 142

THE STORY OF VERNON AND IRENE CASTLE (1939). Irene dancing to "The Yama Yama Man"

Castle (Irene was a quarrelsome technical consultant for the production)* were tailor-made for Astaire and Rogers. Especially bucolic are the scenes of their early courtship, with a nervous Astaire making moon-eyes at Rogers in the family parlor. They marry, join forces as a dance team, with Walter Brennan as their confederate. After many disheartening setbacks, they dance in a European night club to resounding acclaim. The Castle Walk becomes the rage and (at this point the film begins to rely on montage sequences and special effects) their fame spreads. One famous shot (from a specially constructed forty-foot tower) shows the duo dancing their way across a map of the United States, with dozens of followers sprouting in their wake.

When World War I arrives, Vernon Castle enlists in the Royal Flying Corps, while Irene works briefly in silent pictures in Hollywood. She is waiting for him at dinner, one evening, when the news arrives that he has been killed in a training session. "He was a hero, sailor," says Walter Brennan, as there is a heart-rending close-up of a teary-eyed Rogers. The last shot in the movie is the last view of Astaire and Rogers for a decade: Vernon, as a shadowy ghost, dancing off into the distance with Irene clinging to his arm. It is an ending that is almost unbearably moving. The movie is historically interesting for the vintage Castle impersonations (including such numbers as "The Yama Yama Man," "By the Light of the Silvery Moon," "Who's Your Lady Friend?," and "Too Much Mustard") but its main timbre is the shimmering resonance of its casting: Fred and Ginger as Vernon and Irene, a coup that was dramatic as well as musical. For Rogers, the movie marked the end of a crucial period of her career and the beginning of an auspicious new phase in the decade ahead.

* Irene Castle was given script and cast approval, and in her book, *Castles in the Air,* she savages the resulting movie bitterly. She did not like Ginger Rogers, nor her (unbobbed) hairdo, nor her clothes. According to the reminiscences of those involved, she nit-picked extraordinarily on the set. Fortunately, an anti-vivisection referendum happened to be on the ballot in California that year, and animal-lover Ms. Castle disappeared during the filming to wholeheartedly join the campaign.

THE STORY OF VERNON AND IRENE CASTLE (1939). The Castles doing the Maxixe

SOLO AND SOARING

After her Astaire "divorce," Ginger Rogers enjoyed a singularly prolific decade, collaborating with a battery of directors who were, if not Hollywood's select, certainly in the second circle of genius. They were Garson Kanin, Gregory La Cava, Lewis Milestone, Sam Wood, Mitchell Leisen, William Dieterle and, arguably among the best, William A. Wellman, Billy Wilder, Frank Borzage, and Leo McCarey. Consequently, her movies during this stretch had a respectable, often exhilarating gloss. And she herself prescribed the assortment, first, as an RKO luminary, and, later, in 1942, as a free agent roaming the orbit of studios. Assiduously, she whittled her image, refusing, in a blow to artifice, to wear make-up for several celebrated films; altering (for the first time) her hair style from movie to movie in a near-manic compulsion to vary the facade; avoiding, but for a few well-considered lapses, any reversion to her tuneful "chorine" past.

Throughout the forties, she was mentioned continually in fan magazines, and producers worked overtime to announce titles for her that never materialized; it was her period of greatest popularity and also the beginning of her decline. In films such as *Lady in the Dark, Weekend at the Waldorf* and *Magnificent Doll,* she became "grand and remote," in the words of Arlene Croce, betraying her proletarian origins to pretension and jewels. But if, in many people's hearts, she could neither betray her past nor surpass her Astaire legend, she did carve an indelible mark on a war-torn decade. She provided, especially in the carefree effulgence of her comedies, a respite from the world and some of the sunnier moments in American films.

Garson Kanin, an erratically shrewd writer-director, guided the actress through a confection entitled *Bachelor Mother.* Norman Krasna, also the scenarist of *Romance in Manhattan,* scripted, and Krasna was a screenwriter whose career showed an obsession with comic themes of mistaken identity. Thus, Rogers played Polly Parrish, a shop clerk in a huge department store, who, one day on her lunch hour, discovers a foundling on the steps of an orphanage. Despite her protests, she finds herself wrongly identified as the baby's mother, both by the well-meaning orphan-tenders and the playboy son of the store owner. The latter, played amiably enough by David Niven, coddles the "errant" mother by securing her job; then, when she tries unceremoniously to rid herself of the infant by presenting the child to his butler, he scolds her, lectures

BACHELOR MOTHER (1939). With David Niven (seated)

her, and ultimately falls in love with her. Which is providential, considering he is himself mistaken for the "bachelor father" during the laughable commotion.

The cast is first-rate: Charles Coburn, who plays the store magnate with his usual skill, is uproariously certain that his wayward son has produced the brat in question. "I don't care who the father is!" he shouts during one especially confused moment, convinced that the toddler bears a familial resemblance. "*I'm* the grandfather!" And Frank Albertson, always delectably repugnant, has a sharp bit as an opportunistic floorwalker, Rogers' would-be boyfriend, who, out of some imagined revenge, dispatches an anonymous missive to Coburn implicating son Niven in the liaison. Some undeniably amusing business ensues: Niven, reading instructions from a manual on baby care, suggests rubbing gauze spread with oatmeal on the baby's navel, not realizing that two pages are stuck together and he is merging two rather disparate prescriptions; and two different "fathers," one hired by Rogers and one engaged by Niven, appear simultaneously to

BACHELOR MOTHER (1939). With Charles Coburn, Elbert Coplen, Jr., and David Niven

persuade the unflappable Coburn that his son is not the mysterious sire. To no avail.

Hailed in its day as a precious comedy, *Bachelor Mother* wears slightly today as a wonderful premise that fails to fully deliver on its promise, while retaining a lively and infectious quality. The movie is cleanly photographed by Robert De Grasse, yeoman of the RKO lot, and briskly directed, with an eye for small touches, by Kanin. But the jokes are intermittent and telegraphed, and little of the sheer revelry of such a preposterous situation is sustained. Yet Rogers, in her first major solo, gives a balanced, rich, and rewarding performance, shifting easily from moods of youthful impiety (including a quick jitterbug in a dance contest with partner Albertson) to, in her sequences with the baby, a delicate sense of the maternal instinct. This is also the movie which boasts her near-famous pidgin-Swedish masquerade. With Niven as escort, she attends an opulent dinner ball, posing as a foreigner who can't speak a word of English. She chatters merrily and unintelligibly throughout dinner, under the watchful glare of Niven's jealous steady girlfriend. The girl, thinking the "Swede" cannot understand the vernacular, acidly comments aloud upon her departure, "Personally, I'd just as soon go stag," to which Rogers swiftly and unexpectedly replies, "You could, too, with those shoulders!" It is this very sparkle with which she endows the entire film, belying the obvious hokum and transforming the nonsense into jolly entertainment.

Fifth Avenue Girl, directed by Gregory La Cava in 1939, was equally spotty, comparably inviting in spite of its flaws. The muddled story: Walter Connolly, the harassed owner ("I'm really not a capitalist, I'm a victim of the capitalist system!") of Amalgamated Pump, Inc., is neglected in his own home by his society-minded wife, his polo-playing son, and his daffy daughter. On his lonely birthday, he strolls forlornly through Central Park and discovers Rogers, out of work but chipper, who gladly agrees to help him celebrate the occasion. They wine, dine, and dance

FIFTH AVENUE GIRL (1939). With Tim Holt

the night away on a champagne spree which makes the newspaper headlines. Rogers is resigned to being a one-night Cinderella, but Connolly persuades her to stay on as a guest, and set his wayward family right. Whereupon Miss Fixit domesticates the wife, turns the son into a responsible businessman, and straightens out the daughter's tangled love life.

Stylishly directed (watch for a shot through a champagne glass) by La Cava, who achieved a tone that succeeded where the script failed, *Fifth Avenue Girl* attempts to be genial but has an inexplicably cold, vicious undertow that is affronting. A chauffeur, a brutal caricature, rails against "capitalist scum," delivers wild-eyed revolutionary speeches, and is then maneuvered, incredibly, into a wedding with the nutty daughter (and a petit bourgeois shop ownership) at the finale; and Tim Holt is presented as an arrogant, unlikable playboy-son who, for reasons clear only to the scenarist, Allan Scott, lands Rogers for life at the movie's befuddled end.

Sad, because the film is prime at the outset but slips steadily downhill. Walter Connolly, who is a most adorable fat cat, has a particularly memorable rendezvous with Rogers in Central Park. She is munching an apple as he approaches to innocently inquire, "Are you on a diet?" "Yes," she replies defensively, eyeing the stranger, "but against my wishes." They are surprisingly sweet together, whether discussing the irrelevant behavior of seals or cruising on their giddy, drunken whirl in the posh nightclub. There, she displays her scorn for the high-brow clientele by mock-peevishly guarding her purse from possible pickpockets in the crowd. She gives a knowing, free-wheeling performance, but her role is ruinously reduced, after this favorable beginning, to a few transitory passages before the camera. What, after all, is there to say about a movie whose moral is, inanely, "I guess rich people are just poor people with money"?

The following year, La Cava also helmed *Primrose Path,* which was based loosely on the novel *February Hill* by Victoria Lincoln and the play by Robert L. Buckner and Walter Hart. The rather touching story explores the travail of a teen-aged girl from a shantytown address who is cursed with a vinegary grandmother (Queenie Vassar), an urchin sister (Joan Carroll), a drunkard father (Miles Mander) and a mother (Marjorie Rambeau) who moonlights as a "paid companion" to bankroll the brood. The young woman meets a devil-may-care garage mechanic at a local beach diner who charms her and consents to marriage; but, ashamed of her family, she lies about her

PRIMROSE PATH (1940). With Joel McCrea

background and, when he discovers the truth, they quarrel and separate. (They reunite, of course, at the finis, and resolve to untangle the family problems together.) A synopsis hardly does justice to the spell woven by La Cava and, especially, by the evocative photography of Joseph August. The cast is uniformly excellent: Marjorie Rambeau, garnering an Academy Award nomination for her unusually sympathetic portrait of the mother; Queenie Vassar as the embittered, man-hating grandmother; Henry Travers, swelling a cameo role as a benevolent father surrogate; and, particularly, Joel McCrea, one of the screen's best light comedians, as the boyfriend. Marred by contrived difficulties which intrude on the narrative at midway, *Primrose Path* is, regardless, a thoughtful and bewitching excursion into naturalistic comedy-drama.

Rogers is first sighted as a tomboy: with brunette hair, pig-tails, knee socks, and sweat shirt, a sexless outfit she wears deliberately to avoid the stares of adolescent romeos. On her happy-go-lucky way to go clam digging she encounters the equally self-assured McCrea, a part-time lunch-counter clerk who trails her to the beach and steals a kiss; she, having never been kissed before, then follows him to his waterfront night-club haunt and feigns suicide to prompt a marriage proposal. There is an exquisite and sensual chemistry between these two players: McCrea, springy and off-handish, was, with Cary Grant, perhaps her most complementary co-star after Astaire. Their amorous scenes, atmospherically photographed, are touching and tender; and their crazy banter (while one-upping each other as waiter and waitress at the beach café) is captivating and gamey. So, although the movie ends on a sober note, and despite the excesses of the script—an accidental shooting of the mother, a low current of racism toward "Portugee gals", McCrea's contrived outrage over the deception—the two principals, both crisp and enchanting, shoulder the vagaries admirably.

Lewis Milestone, whose reputation tended more toward bathos, directed *Lucky Partners* (1940), an airy, buoyant comedy which pairs Ronald Colman (seemingly an odd choice) with Rogers for felicitous results. Rogers plays a bookstore clerk engaged to an insurance salesman (Jack Carson), who runs into a streak of good luck when she meets a vagabond Greenwich Village artist (Colman). When they finagle some money from a shared sweepstakes ticket, he proposes that they go off together as "brother and sister" on a trip "with no consequences and no regrets." He wants her to see what life is like before she settles into marriage. Incredibly, she accepts and they depart for a visit to Niagara Falls where, as these things must, platonism withers away. Colman runs scared, is arrested, and a wrangle in a smalltown court reveals his true identity: He is an artist once jailed for an "indecent" illustration which has since become a classic and "is even recommended at universities." Now he shuns society out of wounded pride. But Colman interrogates himself, à la *Duck Soup,* and confesses his love for Rogers before the magistrate, so the mess concludes cheerfully.

The light-headed ensemble includes Spring Byington as Rogers' employer-friend, and Carson (in horn-rimmed glasses) as the blustering, jilted beau. Carson turns out to be a gentlemanly loser, however, just one example of the abnormal good nature that pervades this matinée diversion. The final courtroom sequence, presided over by a benign and bemused Harry Davenport, is an uncommon joy. And Colman and Rogers are well matched: he,

LUCKY PARTNERS (1940). With Ronald Colman

KITTY FOYLE (1940). With Ernest Cossart

KITTY FOYLE (1940). In the title role

roguish, gallant, and whimsical, supremely confident in his bachelorhood; she, earthbound and disingenuous, suspecting the worst.

"I knew it was a colorful, adult role, the sort of thing for which I was constantly looking to shake off this image of a girl who has danced her way to success," said Rogers of her next part in *Kitty Foyle* (1940), "but I didn't think it was for me." Though she originally rejected the archetypal white-collar heroine of Christopher Morley's popular novel, subtitled *The Natural History of a Woman,* she was eventually persuaded to play the role by producer David Hempstead. Dalton Trumbo's screenplay was not equal to the challenge, however, and Morley's book was transformed from a class profile of a "nine-to-five" career to the theatrical account of an ill-fated romance. The class contradictions were lightly brushed in; evidences of her occupation (and private life) were scarcely mentioned. Perhaps because the movie was directed by Sam Wood, a competent but mechanical taskmaster, it lacked any of the bite or fury the treatment deserved.

The story unfolded in flashback as Rogers argued with her mirror "self" over the merits of two prospective lovers: James Craig, an estimable doctor whose proposal she has accepted, and Dennis Morgan, a wealthy Philadelphia scion from her past, who is married and unable to get a divorce, but offers to sail away with her to Europe. The flashback reveals that Morgan, in fact, had once married her but then abandoned her under pressure from his parents (who cannot abide the thought of a lowborn relative), leaving her to fend for herself and their impending baby, who died in childbirth.

Sensibly, at the story's conclusion, Rogers chooses Craig, since the Production Code wouldn't have tolerated any other decision; neither, surely, would have moviegoers since Morgan is such a pathetic, nondescript hero. And Craig is likewise lame, two reasons why the movie is less than meets the eye. Rogers was fine: understated, honest, strong, and alluring. She was honored with an Academy Award (her only), a tribute she really deserved cumulatively rather than for this adequate romantic drama, in a year with tough competition. "This is," she announced tearfully at the ceremony, "the happiest moment of my life."*

Garson Kanin's *Tom, Dick and Harry,* released in 1941, has its fierce admirers, now and then, in-

*Her competition for the Oscar in 1940 was Bette Davis (*The Letter*), Joan Fontaine (*Rebecca*), Katharine Hepburn (*The Philadelphia Story*), and Martha Scott (*Our Town*). There was some sentiment in Hollywood to nominate Rogers for her performance in *Primrose Path* instead, but to no avail.

TOM, DICK AND HARRY (1941). With George Murphy

cluding Otis Ferguson, who called it "a honey of a picture." Kanin, who had a flair for fantasy, contributed perhaps his finest directorial credit with this fanciful yarn about a phone operator (played, to almost unbearably flighty proportions, by a dark-haired Rogers) who agrees in a daze to marry three ardent suitors. Of the three, gogetter auto salesman Tom (George Murphy) is earnest but stodgy; handsome millionaire Dick (Alan Marshal) is of purely visual interest; and only dreamy idealist Harry (Burgess Meredith) who opines, "I don't believe in this every-man-for-himself; I get lonesome," is worth doting on. Their "date" on $1.85—dancing in the listening booth of a local phonograph store, a spin at the bowling alley, a frosty-breath offer of marriage on the moonlit porch, and, miraculously, the tiny tinkle of bells when they kiss—is a sequence for wistful lovers of all ages. In a last-minute reversal, after selecting Dick, she settles on bare-budget Harry when that bell rings again, convincing her that true love cannot go unrequited. (Kanin reportedly kept the ending secret from the cast during shooting.)

The highlights of *Tom, Dick and Harry* are four bizarre, delightful,

ROXIE HART (1942). With George Montgomery

and tantalizingly brief dream reveries (composed by Vernon L. Walker) that forecast young Rogers' predicament were she to marry Tom, Dick, Harry or all three. Nightmarishly gleaming kitchens, screaming tots in gigantic highchairs, a trio of husbands singing "Down By the Old Mill Stream" in the shower—all combine to recommend *Tom, Dick and Harry* as a minor gem of comedy. One footnote: Phil Silvers has an incisive vignette as an ice-cream vendor who complains, "You don't have to yell at me, just because I'm a little obnoxious," when he pokes his mercenary head into the windows of smooch-busy cars.

William Wellman's *Roxie Hart* (1942), is little-seen today, either on television or in revival houses, though it is surely one of her most novel comedies, a slap-happy and, at moments, downright silly movie. Nunnally Johnson contributed the wavering screenplay from the 1926 play, *Chicago,* by Maurine Watkins. Newshound George Montgomery, a bovine sort of actor, opens the movie by stumbling into a Chicago saloon to lament the good old days of murder scoops and, especially, "the prettiest woman ever tried for murder in Cook County." A flashback to the twenties introduces Roxie, a curly-haired, gum-chewing flapper (an unusually boisterous performance by Rogers) who is persuaded by a misanthropic reporter (Lynne Overman) and a theatrical agent (Nigel Bruce) to become famous overnight by being arrested for the shooting of her lover. They see that her picture, with ample coverage of her knees, is splashed across the city's front pages, in well-considered poses with the "stiff" and her sheepish husband.

Enter Adolphe Menjou, a slick mouthpiece who prefers his clients guilty, but makes an exception in Roxie's case. When an equal-rights movement among women's clubs demands that Roxie, and all women, be hanged for their monstrous crimes, the trial assumes an ominous portent for the publicity-seeker. The uproarious climax—with a mock-plaintive Roxie mouthing rehearsed lies; a jury of peers who, as the name suggests, peer at Roxie's legs, "her best defense"; and a tour de force defense by Menjou, who climaxes his argument by catching Roxie in a faint, hoisting her prostrate form before the judge and announcing, "The defense rests!"—alone offsets the excesses of Wellman's burlesque. At its best, though, his direction sweetly evokes the bygone era, with tasty bits of character and humor. Memorable gag: After hearing a plea for legal funds from Roxie's husband, her father, a hayseed farmer, sits rocking slowly and unconcernedly in his chair. Then he turns to Mrs. Hart, who is knitting nearby. "They're going to hang Roxie," he says in a matter-of-fact voice. "What did I tell you?" she replies stoically, and the scene fades. As Roxie, Rogers, who is almost too bawdy, has two short dances, a black bottom and a tap dance, both choreographed by Hermes Pan, neither very elaborate nor grand. But she is uncommonly sprightly in this movie, nonetheless, and it is a shame to see her, in the movie's postscript, forlornly wed to Montgomery and coping with a brood of screaming brats.

Box-office duty: *Tales of Manhattan,* directed by Julien Duvivier for Twentieth Century-Fox in 1942, was patterned after Paramount's *If I Had a Million* in 1932 or, even earlier, Marshall Neilan's *Bits of Life* in 1921, with its all-star, multi-story concept. The protagonist, oddly, was a full-dress suit which is pursued by the camera lens through four segments and an epilogue (an additional segment, with W. C. Fields, Margaret Dumont and Phil Silvers, was deleted from the release print), as it changes hands and fortunes, beginning as the garb for a Broadway matinée idol and concluding as the ragged scarecrow in a "Negro" farmer's field. Rogers appeared in segment two of this bon-bon, a weak comedy interlude in an otherwise solemn context, with Roland

TALES OF MANHATTAN (1942). With Cesar Romero

THE MAJOR AND THE MINOR (1942). With Stanley Andrews and Emory Parnell

Young, Cesar Romero, and Henry Fonda. She, in a striking brunette pageboy, is an engaged young woman who switches her emotions to the shy Fonda. Among others in the "name" cast were Charles Boyer, Rita Hayworth, Charles Laughton, Edward G. Robinson, Ethel Waters, and Paul Robeson. And among the crew of writers, whose individual traits vanished in the labyrinth of plots, were Ben Hecht, Donald Ogden Stewart, and Lamar Trotti.

Billy Wilder was still an unknown quantity as a director in 1942, when Rogers approved him as her mentor for *The Major and the Minor,* so she can be duly credited with launching one of Hollywood's best directors, as well as wisely approving one of her most enchanting vehicles. The hypothesis was "on the verge of the impossible," in Wilder's words, "but there was that willing suspension of shocked disbelief." She actually donned three masks: playing herself, a "child" of twelve ("After all," says Wilder, "this was 1941") and her mother Lela, who also appeared (her only such appearance) in cameo in the movie. She is perhaps the only actress in

THE MAJOR AND THE MINOR (1942). With Ray Milland

Hollywood who could have borne such utter whimsy—in this wacky fiction of a career woman who wearies of the metropolis, and poses as a "little kid" to ride half-fare on the train home to Iowa—without becoming excessively coy.

The story begins with Susan Applegate (Rogers), disillusioned with New York and particularly put off by the lecherous behavior of one Robert Benchley in a hotel suite, deciding to return home to Stevenson, Iowa. When she discovers that she lacks sufficient money for the train fare, she rearranges her hair into pigtails—looking amazingly youthful—"lifts" a balloon from a nearby kiddie, and persuades a telephone grifter to pose as her "daddy" at the ticket booth. Though she sings "A Tisket, A Tasket," aboard the locomotive, the lunk-headed trackmen think "she looks kind of filled-out for twelve." With exasperated patience, she explains that she has gland trouble and, furthermore, her family derives from big-boned Swedish stock. The ruse perishes, however, when she is seen reading *Esquire* and, later, smoking cigarettes furtively on the open-air deck. Chased by the trainmen, she somehow winds up in a compartment with Ray Milland, an army major en route to his military college and, not incidentally, his fiancée. Milland, apparently, is unworldly enough to believe that she is of a prepubescent age. She calls him Uncle Phillip; he calls her Su-Su. And yet, Lolitan shades of Nabokov, he has these strange longings toward the "little kid."

At any rate—skipping over some not-unwarranted jealousy by Rita Johnson, the major's fiancée, and a tough-minded vignette by the fiancée's sister, young Diana Lynn, who really *is* twelve—"Su-Su" Applegate sojourns with the major to the military academy. There she is attacked by an onslaught of sex-starved cadets who each, in the order of rank, instruct her regarding the "Maginot Line" offensive tactics, one of the most dizzy comedic sequences of the forties. Her sights, of course, are set on the major but—after a turn at tap dancing, and a showdown with the disagreeable fiancée—she leaves the army post, still a child in the major's befogged mind. He, notwithstanding, has been nettled by the experience, and his impending marriage collapses.

En route to a new army appointment, he pauses in Stevenson, Iowa, to pay his respects to little Su-Su. There, moviegoers catch their only celluloid peek at Lela Rogers, who is rocking on the Applegate front porch, with a blur of moths swirling about her lamp. Rogers, Jr., hearing of the major's approach, dons mama's glasses and apron and streaks her hair gray—the effect is of astonishing

ONCE UPON A HONEYMOON (1942). With Cary Grant

physical similarity—to learn, in her conversation with the unsuspecting major, that his intended marriage is kaput. Then she changes, packs, and hustles down to the train station where, during a beautifully photographed finale, she gives him her "Maginot Line" and things conclude blissfully. They, the soft-mannered Milland and a lovably childish Rogers, were as aptly partnered as Wilder and co-scenarist Charles Brackett; and, in the convergence of the four paths, one of filmdom's headier "screwball" comedies was devised.

Nearly as frolicsome, in a seriocomic vein, was *Once Upon a Honeymoon,* Leo McCarey's oddball and uneven movie of 1942, which signaled, momentarily, Rogers' return to the RKO lot. "Mr. McCarey has produced a callous film," Bosley Crowther wrote in *The New York Times,* reflecting the popular view of the day, "It is a very strange and stark lark." Yet, similar in concept to Charlie Chaplin's *The Great Dictator* or Ernst Lubitsch's *To Be or Not To Be,* McCarey's movie is a black comedy of some magnetism

TENDER COMRADE (1943). With Richard Martin and Kim Hunter

today, despite its lapses. McCarey, who later with his anti-communist *My Son John* confirmed that his political instincts were crude, discovered a golden duo in Cary Grant and Rogers who at least partially offset the heavy-handed theatrics of *Once Upon a Honeymoon*. Their early sequences together are superb, as he, a crack newsman, pursues her across the map of Europe, trying to persuade her that her husband (an oily performance by Walter Slezak) is a "finger man" for Hitler, who, after each country he visits, betrays the government to an invasion of storm troopers. Despite the spotty nature of the script, which seriously strained the comic momentum by leaping from Vienna (set in 1938) to Scandinavia to France, with ample references to the plight of Jews, Grant, the superlative light comedian of the screen, uplifted the undertaking. He was totally disarming, even in so serious a framework.

Rogers, who was rarely cast opposite such a refined performer, filled a winsome role as a burlesque queen (a return to type) from America, a gold digger who marries dignitary Slezak. Though lowborn and Irish, she occasionally masquerades as a patrician; at one point in the film, she even executes a speedy cluster of dialects—always her specialty. In the course of the story, she must switch her emotions as well as her political impulses, and she handles both difficult transitions dexterously.

Tender Comrade—that ill-fated property directed by Edward Dmytryk and written by Dalton Trumbo, both later hounded by HUAC—was actually an innocuous patriotic propaganda piece with Rogers colorlessly cast as the dedicated war-wife of Robert Ryan. She organizes a group of women co-workers from Douglas Aircraft factory into a co-operative boardinghouse cell in Los Angeles. "We could run the joint like a democracy," she suggests, sparing any subtlety in the wartime allegory. "And if anything comes up we could take a vote." Events do "come up," particularly, one spouse who is less than loyal, but Rogers, in a cold, domineering performance, tightly guides the ship (of state) of matrimony. Russell Metty's exceptional photography is squandered in a stagy, bombastic, sentimentalized story that is studded with prewar flashbacks, each introduced by the recurring panorama of two lovers (Rogers and Ryan) standing in embrace on a clouded horizon. At the climax, which doesn't arrive soon enough, Rogers is informed that Ryan has succumbed on the battlefield. She cradles her baby, born in father's absence, and holds aloft Ryan's framed portrait. "Little guy, you two aren't ever going to meet," she says mournfully. "He went out and died so you can have a better break when you grow up than he ever had. Don't ever let anybody say he died for nothing." Then she descends the house stairs to stoically continue with life and, presumably, democracy. One marvels that the bantam minds of HUAC perceived subversion in such a superficial melodrama.*

She reached the peak of her career, and began her slow decline, with *Lady in the Dark*, released the next year, a gaudy, lavish, but badly flawed filmization of the Broadway hit. "Ginger Rogers' days of top stardom ended with this film," David Chierichetti writes in *Hollywood Director*, "and what should have been the crowning achievement of Mitchell Leisen's career ended up to be just another picture."** She lobbied actively to play the role, which Gertrude Lawrence had played to resounding acclaim on the stage, as part of her three-picture deal with Paramount that began with *The Major and the Minor*. And though the semi-musical, scripted by Moss Hart and scored by Kurt Weill and Ira Gershwin, was successful at the box office, it is easily one of the most miscalculated extravaganzas ever committed to celluloid, troubled from brooding conception to disputed execution.

The story: Liza Elliott, a brittle, domineering top fashion editor, undergoes psychoanalysis to cure her mercurial moods, and is told by her psychiatrist (Barry Sullivan) that she privately desires to be more feminine. This is the cue for three outrageously ostentatious dream sequences in which she is haunted by the men in her life, Ray Milland (her abrasive associate editor), Warner Baxter (her financial "angel," who is seeking a divorce in order to marry her) and Jon Hall (a vain movie star). One of the sleep-visions occurs in a sea of blue, as she poses for a new postage stamp. Another, colored in gold, conjures a fantastic, unwanted wedding with Baxter. The third, and final dream, imagines a surrealistic, circus-like world in which she is brought before a tribunal to choose between her youthful self and her garishly glamorized self. These sequences, in three-strip Technicolor, are technically ambitious, with enthralling lighting, color tones, and elaborate costumes, many suggested by director Leisen. But the wrinkles in *Lady in the Dark* are

*Ginger Rogers demonstrated her patriotism in other ways during World War II, including USO outings and military short subjects. Among her wartime featurettes were *Safeguarding Military Information*, narrated with Walter Huston, *Battle Stations*, narrated with Spencer Tracy and directed by Garson Kanin, and the five-minute *Ginger Rogers Finds a Bargain*, advancing the cause of War Loans.

**David Chierichetti, *Hollywood Director*, Curtis Books, 1973, p. 195.

symbolized by the excision of the well-known song, "My Ship," ruthlessly cut from the final print by producer B. G. DeSylva, over the protests of Leisen—a critical deletion since, in the story, the tune is supposed to have psychically distressed her since childhood. Overlong and overblown, the movie also, curiously, lost something vital and urgent in the translation from stage to screen.

Rogers—though she faithfully delivered the show's songs, including "Saga of Jenny"—offered a stilted and exaggerated performance, a rare complaint. "It soon became apparent," Chierichetti writes, "that Ginger Rogers' singing and dancing were fine, but her acting failed to capture all the nuances and ambiguities of Liza Elliott's complex psyche, so that the visual aspects of the film assumed greater importance in Leisen's scheme of things as he tried to convey certain dramatic points."* Leisen, a stylish if minor director, complained to Chierichetti, before his death in 1972, that Rogers often appeared late on the set and, one particular day, when the "Suddenly It's Spring" number was due to be lensed, she arrived in the late afternoon, stalling 165 electricians all day. Leisen also recalled, somewhat bitterly, that she married (husband three Jack Briggs) during the shooting "and the entire company just sat there for two weeks" while they honeymooned. "She was very bad at matching action," Leisen continued, offering an unusual insight into her creative limitations. "You take a master shot first and then you go in and

**Hollywood Director*, p. 190.

LADY IN THE DARK (1944). With Ray Milland

I'LL BE SEEING YOU (1944). With Joseph Cotten

make up your close-ups. If she lights a cigarette on a certain line in the master take, it has to be lit on exactly that word in the close-up. Otherwise, you can't cut it together. She always had a hard time remembering how she'd done it."*

The actress was meanwhile exploring a number of options: an independent partnership with RKO executive Charles Koerner; and a version of Margaret Runbeck's *Great Answer*, the 1944 novel about a newspaperwoman, for her own Lincoln Productions. These ventures didn't materialize, unfortunately, so she signed on loan-out to Selznick Productions for *I'll Be Seeing You*, an unpretentious little jewel with checkered roots. The picture was almost vetoed by magnate David O. Selznick, but producer

***Hollywood Director*, p. 196.

Dore Schary received the go-ahead after Rogers agreed to play the principal role. Then, Schary quarreled with director William Dieterle during shooting, and actually directed a few scenes himself before Dieterle returned to the set. But despite the hubbub—and despite a nonexistent reputation among buffs today—*I'll Be Seeing You* is a tender, tactful, and sweet-natured film with first-rate production values and a host of harmonious performances.

Rogers plays a reformatory parolee who, as a flashback reveals, is innocent of a manslaughter charge. She meets a soldier on Christmas furlough (sensitively played by Joseph Cotten) who is spooked by memories of combat. They fall in love and she helps him to overcome his mental persecution, though she knows that she herself, whatever her feelings, must return to prison at the end of the holidays. Originally titled *Double Furlough* and retitled for a popular song which was purchased for use in the movie, the film was not only timely, but, with the finely etched sincerity of Rogers and Cotten, also quite affecting. Especially right are the instances of small-town life depicted by Dieterle, such as a simple-hearted family dinner at

WEEKEND AT THE WALDORF (1945). With Walter Pidgeon

HEARTBEAT (1946). With Adolphe Menjou

MAGNIFICENT DOLL (1946). With David Niven

Yuletide with plum pudding, neighborly conversation and a group singalong of "Oh, Come All Ye Faithful." The family, anyone's envy, are Tom Tully as the understanding Mr. Marshall; Spring Byington as his wife, an ethereal presence of goodwill; and Shirley Temple in a major teen-aged role as the blundering adolescent of the clan, who is suspicious of "jailbird" Rogers. With scarcely a false note and marred only by two quick voice-over psychic apparitions experienced by Cotten, the movie evolves to its sober end, with Cotten, restored to health, bidding Rogers a teary, temporary farewell at the prison gate as she enters to serve the remainder of her six-year term.

Weekend at the Waldorf, directed by Robert Z. Leonard for MGM in 1945, was a slick entertainment of little moment. Vicki Baum's *Grand Hotel* was revamped, with Rogers in the Greta Garbo guise, as an all-star vehicle for the likes of Walter Pidgeon, Van Johnson, Robert Benchley, Edward Arnold, Xavier Cugat, and others. Lana Turner, miscast as a stenographer who falls in love with war-wounded Johnson, was also among the "guests" in this overlong, watered-down advertisement for the Waldorf. As for Rogers, she was cast as a disconsolate movie star who is kept busy by her wardrobe changes: twelve Irene gowns and multiple Sydney Guilaroff coiffures. Inevitably, she too falls in love—with cynical war correspondent Pidgeon. Their few scenes together are the only pale relief from this perfunctory movie, the first, ignobly, to invest her persona with such affluence and self-importance.*

Two offbeat entries in 1946: *Heartbeat* and *Magnificent Doll.* The former, again directed by the workmanlike Sam Wood, who possessed little of the quirkiness the property demanded, concerned a young pickpocket (Rogers) who falls in love with a young diplomat, played by Jean-Pierre Aumont, at a plush embassy ball in Paris. Their romance is rather tedious, as romances go, and Rogers is limited, in her part, to mugging. The early scenes are better, especially with a haughty Basil Rathbone presiding over a motley school of pickpockets; and the minor characters—Adolphe Menjou as an ambassador, Mikhail Rasumny as a pickpocket pal—are thankfully expert. But it would be generous to describe this marriage of *Oliver* and *Pygmalion* as a fizzle. It would be Rogers' last appearance under the RKO logo for ten years.

Magnificent Doll, directed by

*By 1945, then thirty-four years old, Ginger Rogers was the highest-paid Hollywood star, earning $292,159, a sum which was reportedly the eighth biggest salary in the United States.

IT HAD TO BE YOU (1947). With Cornel Wilde and Bill Walker

Frank Borzage for Universal, is a biography of Dolly Madison with Rogers intriguingly cast as the former First Lady. Borzage, whose heart was in the right place even when his mind was elsewhere, was a primitive romanticist whose best films (*Man's Castle, Three Comrades*) are spellbinding love stories set in the discord of a hostile world. In this instance, Borzage was handicapped by the Irving Stone script, which posited Rogers as the lover of Aaron Burr. He, in a gambit the history books missed, yields his claims to the presidency because Dolly Madison dissuades him. Told in flashback, the movie skims over her childhood on her father's plantation in Virginia, her first unhappy marriage, her liaison with Burr, and her remarriage to James Madison, ending in the period of Jefferson's presidency while Madison is still the Secretary of State. Extravagant sets and costumes, plus a valid score by Harry J. Salter, hardly alleviated a scenario which was, in the words of Bosley Crowther, inauthentic "pompous twaddle." Burgess Meredith (as a Utopian James Madison) and David Niven (as a villainous Aaron Burr) did buoy the picture somewhat. But Rogers, in the terse words of *Time* magazine, was "forced into a role above her head and a script that is beneath it." She was on unfamiliar and shaky ground. David Niven, in his autobiography, dismissed the script as "gibberish" and kindly termed the Rogers-Niven (Dolly Madison-Aaron Burr) coupling as "the two most unlikely bits of casting of the century."

Travesty followed history with *It Had To Be You,* directed by Don Hartman and cameraman Rudolph Maté for Columbia in 1947. The story, which exploited the two unseemly emerging tendencies in the "adult" Rogers heroine, wealth and neuroses, began where *Tom, Dick and Harry* left off. She is a daft heiress, a sculptress by profession, who has jilted three grooms in succession. So unreliable are her marriage plans that the father of intended-husband number four remarks, "The boys at the club are laying five to one this one also won't go through." Why such vacillation? It seems, according to the absurd story (concocted by Hartman and Allen Boretz), that she is so afflicted by the memory of the first "sweetheart" of her childhood, a six-year-old kid in an Indian outfit, that an imaginary dream lover in Indian clothing keeps turning up in her imagination. So she has an "Injun complex." That is cue enough for Cornel Wilde, who, though he is a New York fireman, happens to approximate the dream lover. More screwy than screwball, *It Had To Be You* is only periodically rosy, but the practiced players acquit themselves well under the shoestring circumstances.

Postscript: *The Barkleys of*

THE BARKLEYS OF BROADWAY (1949). With Oscar Levant, Fred Astaire, Clinton Sundberg, and Gale Robbins

Broadway (1949), directed by Charles Walters from a script by Betty Comden and Adolph Green, marked the grand reunion of Fred Astaire and Ginger Rogers. The movie was a throwback to an earlier decade, another era, besides being a tongue-in-cheek summation of their variable partnership. It nearly didn't happen. Shooting had already begun, the dances were already set, when Judy Garland collapsed on the MGM lot (from the grueling rehearsals, some said) and Rogers was summoned from her sprawling ranch in Oregon to play the tailor-made role of Dinah Barkley, the female half of a famed dancing duo who bicker incessantly in their private life as husband and wife. She has a yen to be a "serious" actress (the real-life parallel is obvious), and is tempted to part from the dancing life by a handsome, sober-minded playwright (Jacques François). He casts her in his new highbrow play, which allows Rogers an opportunity for a too-shrill mimicry of Sarah Bernhardt reciting "La Marseillaise." Josh Barkley, meanwhile, is forced by the abrupt turn of events to recon-

THE BARKLEYS OF BROADWAY (1949). Fred and Ginger dancing to "Manhattan Downbeat"

sider his hoofing wife in a new, equitable light. The MGM production was glossy and pat, lacking both the warts and the spontaneity of the RKO Astaire-Rogers features; the movie offered a subdued Oscar Levant, for example, as the merged substitute for Eric Blore and Edward Everett Horton, while furnishing Josh and Dinah with fame, fortune, and glittering clothes, a device which had the effect of lessening the interest while heightening the verity. Still, *The Barkleys of Broadway* is not disastrous, simply disappointing. And its choice sequences are really quite splendid.

The movie begins with, appropriately, a dance, "Swing Trot," a brassy, upbeat number performed, unfortunately, over the titles. They are a lovey team in the limelight, the story reveals, but they are all barbs, snarls, and cut glass off the stage. Their perennial argument—over who is the senior inspiration of the duo—erupts finally when an avant-garde Latvian artist unveils a painting in their honor, depicting Josh as a frying pan and she as the formless batter which is molded by his Svengalian genius. "You couldn't walk across a stage without me," argues Astaire, with words that reverberate with irony into the well of film history. "There isn't a gesture that you do that you didn't learn from me." She stonily replies: "You've been taking me for granted too. I have to stand on my own two feet as a person and as an actress." When they separate at midway in the narrative—having, until that point, achieved a subtle equality that is echoed in the movie's theme—*The Barkleys of Broadway* crumbles at the seams.

The musical routines are sharp: "You'd Be Hard to Replace," a pleasant ballad; "My One and Only Highland Fling," which has a deadpanned Astaire in kilts, Rogers likewise, she rolling her r's ferociously and both singing in a Scottish accent and dancing jauntily; "Bouncin' the Blues," an explosive rehearsal jog; "Shoes With Wings On," Astaire's near-classic as a cobbler who is bewitched by dozens of pairs of animated shoes; and, of course, the reprise of "They Can't Take That Away From Me" from the earlier *Shall We Dance*. To this day, Rogers contends that the idea for including the nostalgic song was hers. She, then thirty-eight, and Astaire, then fifty-nine, briefly returned to form, again conjuring the magic in a number that was, in the words of Arlene Croce, an "old smoothie turn." It was their farewell to a seemingly less complicated time and, for Rogers, her hello to another decade, a different world, an industry in flux, and a future of change.

FOREVER GINGER: THE LAST TWO DECADES

Middle age is a well-traveled route for the screen actress, meaning "marriage," perhaps, and a "family"; a higher incidence of melodramas and a smaller frequency of comedies; fewer roles, smaller roles, and an eventual disappearance into the limbo of retirement. Such is the Hollywood way. After two decades in the movies, Ginger Rogers was on the verge of a precipitous descent into that limbo; and the industry, too—beset by television, political troubles, and antitrust proceedings—was not at its former glory. That she worked as steadily as she did during the fickle decade of the fifties is a tribute to her will to survive. And, though her post-1949 credits are laced with pablum, at least one film—Howard Hawks' *Monkey Business*—is choice, showing, conclusively, that Rogers had the will but screenland had lost the way.

She greeted the new decade at Warner Brothers, appearing, in 1950, in *Perfect Strangers,* directed by Bretaigne Windust. The script was borrowed from *Ladies and Gentlemen,* a Ben Hecht-Charles MacArthur play written for Helen Hayes in 1939. Dennis Morgan, the listless co-star of *Kitty Foyle,* again was co-billed as a married man (with two children) who falls in love with Rogers, a divorcée, while both are serving as jurors for a love nest murder trial. The defendant, it seems, had begged his wife for a divorce shortly before she plummeted from a cliff to her death; it requires the strength of her own feelings for Morgan to convince Rogers the man is innocent, and she in turn persuades the skeptical jury. As with *Kitty Foyle,* of course, married-man Morgan and Rogers part resignedly at the movie's end, preserving the niceties of filmdom's mores. Hackneyed and obtuse, the best moments of *Perfect Strangers* belong mainly to the bit players: Thelma Ritter as a dense, pregnant housewife; Harry Bellaver as a loutish bailiff; Margalo Gillmore as an embittered high-society dame whose husband has deserted her. Topnotch production values (including a credible score by Leigh Harline) cannot compensate for the pathetic floundering, though, of script and stars.

The actress remained at Warner Brothers for *Storm Warning,* directed by Stuart Heisler in 1951. It was her solitary foray into the realm of social consciousness, a movie that was a curiously hollow echo of Warners' halcyon days of social responsibility in the early thirties. Perhaps the film was inspired by the flurry of liberal-thinking "race" pictures of the era, movies like Elia Kazan's *Pinky* and

PERFECT STRANGERS (1950). With Dennis Morgan and Harry Bellaver

Joseph L. Mankiewicz's *No Way Out*. Written by Daniel Fuchs and Richard Brooks, the Warners entry was nevertheless individual in its treatment, reminiscent of the earlier *Black Legion*. A blistering indictment of the Ku Klux Klan, if long on theatrics and short on analysis, the movie starred the unlikely trio of Ronald Reagan (later the right-wing Republican governor of California), Doris Day (later a pinup symbol of dauntless virginity) and Rogers.

Rogers was the nominal star, playing an innocent bystander, a model by trade, who arrives at a small, nameless Southern town to visit her sister (Day). The avenues are eerily deserted upon her arrival, and she discovers why when she accidentally witnesses the Klan-directed "execution" of a newsman, an "outsider" who had been working on an exposé. The plot thickens when she later discovers that her sister's husband, played as a stupid bully by Steve Cochran, is one of the killers. Reagan, unexpectedly, was sturdy enough as the intrepid prosecutor who overcomes treachery, a near-rape, and two violent deaths to heroically set things right; and Rogers, whose role was more ploy than character, executed her part neatly. Low-key and grim,

STORM WARNING (1950). With Steve Cochran and Doris Day

Storm Warning is a respectable, serious-minded footnote to her otherwise largely diversionary career.

One of the actress' most negligible titles was *The Groom Wore Spurs,* an independent feature produced by Fidelity Pictures for Universal-International in 1951 and directed by Richard Whorf. Sloppy, insipid, and grotesquely contrived, the movie concerned a singing movie cowboy (played by ace blowhard Jack Carson) who is actually skittish about horses and can't strum the guitar. His marriage to a lawyer (Rogers) who has come to his aid is quarrelsome, and the couple eventually separate. When Carson is suspected of killing a gambler, the duo is forced to join forces and corral the real murderer in a climactic airport sequence of screeching airplanes that is slapstick comedy at its worst. Joan Davis was lost in the cast as a sympathetic friend, ironically a role that Rogers herself might have filled two decades earlier. The movie itself seemed a reversion, sans music, to the racking banalities of her Paramount period. Rogers gives an exaggerated performance, fluctuating broadly between farce and romance, in a vehicle that is itself tortured beyond credibility.*

Edmund Goulding, a director of some talent, fashioned *We're Not Married,* released by Twentieth Century-Fox the next year, another of those all-star compositions with inconsequential, if happy, merit. The premise is simple: five couples discover that they are really not wed, due to the error of a benign justice of the peace (played by Victor Moore). Rogers and Fred Allen played one of the couples, a radio team who coo together on national hook-up but are crankily married in private life. The other un-marrieds include Eve Arden and Paul Douglas, as a restless suburban couple; Marilyn Monroe, the just-anointed "Mrs. Mississippi," and distraught husband David Wayne; Texas millionaire Louis Calhern and scheming wife Zsa Zsa Gabor, both involved in a messy divorce suit; and soldier Eddie Bracken, who is on the verge of overseas transfer and must remarry expectant wife Mitzi Gaynor before departure. The performances were pungent all around, especially Rogers and Allen (performing a skit similar to the one Allen and Tallulah Bankhead performed often on the radio) as the hypocri-

*Also in 1951, she returned to Broadway to appear in author-director-star Louis Verneuil's *Love and Let Love*. Plagued by Verneuil's illness and unfavorable reviews, the show folded after fifty-six performances.

THE GROOM WORE SPURS (1951). With Joan Davis and Ross Hunter

WE'RE NOT MARRIED (1952). With Fred Allen and Victor Moore

MONKEY BUSINESS (1952). With Cary Grant, Robert Cornthwaite, and Marilyn Monroe

tical couple who, wed acrimoniously for twenty-one years, never speak to each other at home, though, "on the air" with their daily breakfast show, they impersonate the perfect marriage. Goulding's five-cornered comedy was surprisingly well-balanced for its episodic structure, and mirthful besides.

Howard Hawks' *Monkey Business* is, perhaps excepting the Astaire films, the single most satisfying movie in which Rogers ever appeared. It was the perfect vehicle for two aging sex symbols, Cary Grant and Ginger Rogers, and an equally aging master-director, Howard Hawks, for age itself is the ironic subject, reversing, in the words of Arthur Knight, "the general movie view of life, suggesting that there might be some virtue and dignity in maturity, and that the golden dream of eternal youth could have its nightmare aspects." Even Hawks, aware of the excruciating humor of the escapade, has admitted, in interviews, that he might have gone "too far" with the idea, so wild and almost unpleasant does the pranking become.

The story begins slowly, almost unbearably so, in the home of Dr. Barnaby Fulton and his wife, as if to underline the stultifying life embraced by the middle-age marrieds. Fulton, a research chemist, is working on the formula for a youth potion, and he stumbles on the right concoction by accident. When a "guinea" chimpanzee inadvertently mixes the proper proportions, and then deposits the results into the company water cooler, the pace of Hawks' narrative quickens, races, and never brakes. Every time someone is thirsty, he or she drinks from the potent cooler and succumbs to a barbaric fit of giggling adolescence. This includes the Fultons, who discover something important about hallowed youth and their own lives in the process. What a synopsis cannot fairly convey is the havoc wreaked by Hawks, or the layers of meaning he extracts from the Ben Hecht-Charles Lederer-I.A.L. Diamond script. Not to be confused with the Marx Brothers movie of the same name, *Monkey Business* is a riotous revelry of exact and exacting dimensions.

Outstanding moments abound: the lurching auto ride an infantilized Grant takes with buxom secretary Marilyn Monroe; the mix-up which occurs when Edwina (Rogers) believes a real baby, which has crawled into her path, is the scientist himself gone one step too far. Especially outrageous is the conspiracy formed by Grant and George "Foghorn" Winslow, the gravel-voiced child player, to don war paint and scalp a meddling romeo played by Hugh Marlowe. Hawks has loaded the story with lightweight gags (such as Grant's eyesight, which comes and goes with the youth potion) and the cast couldn't be better, including Monroe, who lampoons her own formidable presence, and Charles Coburn as Oliver Oxley, president of the youth-seeking enterprise, who himself imbibes the fluid at the movie's hectic climax.

Grant delivers an agile, inventive, and thoroughly disarming performance as the absent-minded professor who, usually sober and reflective, goes haywire when under the influence. His performance is equaled by Rogers, whose role is similarly demanding, rushing from spasms of jealousy (incurred by the presence of Monroe) to long spells of sedate maturity to raving childish spurts. Their "second honeymoon" fling is a lovely and delirious example of the latter, nicely underplayed by both. When the elixir strikes her, she begins to dance reflexively (as if conjuring the Astaire musicals in her mind) and she has a substantial turn at dancing in *Monkev Business*. In the romantic thread which weaves the story together, she and Grant offer one of the most sensitive and fully rounded sketches of middle-aged matrimony in the comic world of cinema.

Dreamboat, also released by Fox

MONKEY BUSINESS (1952). With Cary Grant

DREAMBOAT (1952). With Clifton Webb in parody of silent film about World War I

in 1952, is one of the more exasperating movies in the Rogers file, simply because its premise is promising while its execution is highly flawed. Clifton Webb plays a mild-mannered English professor at a Midwest college. He is a bookworm, a prude, until, one day, a television program debuts called *The Return of El Toro* which reveals the soft-spoken academician as the former Bruce Blair, a silent-era matinée idol of the screen. His former co-star, Gloria Marlowe, played by Rogers, introduces the immensely popular old-time flickers on the Exotic Perfume Hour. Ridiculed by his students and threatened by the university trustees (except for madame president, who unabashedly throws herself at the feet of the once-dashing star), Webb sojourns to New York City, accompanied by his strait-laced daughter (Anne Francis), to file suit halting the showing of his movies. "After all," he says, arguing for his privacy, "it's not like concealing a criminal record." While in the metropolis, though, his long-term enmity with co-star Rogers is forgotten, he becomes involved in well-publicized scrapes which heighten his heroic stature and, against his own best judgment, he returns triumphantly to Hollywood to star again in "talkies," a coda which is handled in an abrupt and unsatisfying fashion.

The silent-movie parodies, which occur too briefly in *Dreamboat*, are very ingenious and funny, with Webb and Rogers emoting in a World War I flying ace tale, a Foreign Legion shortie, and a Three Musketeer-like costumer, the latter screened in the courtroom finale while the presiding judge munches popcorn. Stinging, too, is the television satire (with Rogers extolling perfumes such as "Double Passion" and "My Five Sins"; with the movies TV-edited so that the hero plugs the sponsor) and the satire of the movie colony itself (Webb admits he ranked second to a police dog in a popularity poll). The trouble with this whimsy, which looks fine on paper, is that Claude Binyon directed his own script in a flat, unimaginative, stuffy style. Webb is unusually crotchety and never fleshes out his role, while the marginal romantic adventures of his daughter amount to a tiresome sub-plot. Rogers, second-billed now in her bejeweled "star" phase, is surely welcome in her abbreviated passes before the camera—she even has a night-club ditty, with tuxedo-clad chorus boys in the background, crooning "You'll Never Know"—but the movie is an unfortunate object lesson in how to misapply talent.

Much, much better, if derivative, was Irving Rapper's *Forever Female*, produced for Paramount in 1953, a handsome, engrossing,

FOREVER FEMALE (1953). With Paul Douglas

bittersweet romantic comedy. The story, which unofficially combined elements of *Sunset Boulevard* and *All About Eve*, featured William Holden as a cynical playwright who is emotionally torn between an impetuous ingénue and a fading stage star (played, of course, by Rogers). Based on a J. M. Barrie play, scripted by Julius J. and Philip G. Epstein, the movie skimmed the backbiting world of the theater, where down-and-out thespians at Sardi's drink to the failure of competing plays.

The plot focuses on mottled producer Paul Douglas' unflinching devotion to his glamorous ex-wife (Rogers, looking gorgeous in a blonde chignon), who is escorted, characteristically, by one aspiring beau after another. Holden, an unproduced playwright who informs her bitchily, "Half the time I thought you were charming, and the other half of the time you thought you were so charming it gave me a queasy feeling in the stomach," presents the gravest romantic challenge to Douglas. Holden tailors a play for her called *Unhappy Holiday* and also loses his heart to the actress. But, though she won't admit it, she is really too old for the leading role. A young, pushy, magnetic, coquettish gamin named Sally Carver (Pat Crowley), a name she changes weekly,

BLACK WIDOW (1954). With George Raft

materializes to chase Holden and the part. The situation is uneasy. Holden and Rogers announce their impending marriage, much to Douglas' chagrin, and the mildly heart-rending climax occurs in New England. Holden is chauffeured by Douglas to a summer-stock theater in Maine, where Clara Mootz (the ingénue's real name) is performing the play exactly as its author intended; and then he is driven to Rogers' secret hideaway nearby where aging star Beatrice Page is rumbling about in well-earned privacy, acting her real, uncosmeticized age. Everyone ends up with his deserved partner, but not without a flood of tears.

Rapper's fluid direction—and the tart one-upping dialogue—contributed to the amusement. Holden is, as usual, caustic and swell-headed, but he is superb as the type. Pat Crowley (billed as a "future" Paramount star, though she quickly vanished) is obnoxious—her worst expletive is "That's the Siamese truth!"—in the most annoyingly consistent manner. Paul Douglas, as the "angel" husband who functions more easily outside the strictures of marriage, is magnificent, rendering believable what is plainly one of the more liberated relationships of filmdom. Though the script backslides with a planned re-marriage at the fade-out, he and Rogers trundle through the entire movie with unmistakable rapport, level talk, and glowing professional technique, evoking, as with *Monkey Business,* a generous image of what it means to grow old. Rogers, who looked two decades younger than Douglas, was awarded one of her finer roles of the miserable decade, a woman who is slightly affected, partly self-absorbed, and deeply worried about the onslaught of wrinkled age but, ultimately, magnanimous to a fault.

Rogers' next film, *Black Widow,* was directed by Nunnally Johnson from his own screenplay in CinemaScope for Fox in 1954. Van Heflin, the nominal star, narrates this threadbare, plodding mystery which tells of a vicious young writer (Peggy Ann Garner) who is discovered dead—and pregnant—in his apartment suite. Though the police accuse him of the deed, since the deceased woman had boasted to her friends of a torrid love affair with an unknown correspondent, he himself knows that the murderer is one of his circle of friends. Among the suspects: Reginald Gardiner, who lives upstairs with his actress-wife Rogers, a sharp-tongued and (it is eventually revealed) unloved star. Competent but unsuspenseful, *Black Widow* boasts a disappointing gallery of former top-liners in cheap dressing. Gene Tierney, for example, is used sparingly as Van Heflin's wife; and George Raft lends a colorless, iron-visaged portrait of a detective whose imperturbable hectoring ultimately solves the crime. Van Heflin himself is pallid. Even Rogers, as the jealousy-wracked killer, is used to little advantage, excepting an outburst of convulsive sobbing and fury at the ending. It is the only moment of vigor in an otherwise slack production.

Twist of Fate, directed by David Miller in 1954, was nothing but a potboiler. The complicated plot concerned a former chorine (Rogers again) who learns that the hard-driving businessman (Stanley Baker) she plans to marry is really a criminal mastermind who has not yet divorced his wife. When she meets a local ceramics artist—the dark-featured Jacques Bergerac, then Rogers' husband, a performer with the subtlety of a statue—her own romantic inclinations are derailed. Crime king Baker mistakes Emil, his own henchman, for Rogers' clandestine lover—the twist of fate—and the web of plots collapses in a finale of fire and death. All the clichés are tabbed: a dying scoundrel's confession clears the air; Rogers trips over a woodpile to land in the artist's loving embrace; an abortive love scene between Bergerac and Rogers is symbolically concluded by the close-up of a phonograph needle idling on the turntable. Only Herbert Lom, in a rather feverish portrait of Emil, the henchman, acquits himself honorably. Rogers is adequate, but could such a stock role be otherwise?*

Of a slightly higher quality was *Tight Spot,* directed for Columbia by Phil Karlson in 1955. Reminiscent in concept to *Roxie Hart*—but grim and suspenseful—the movie featured Rogers as a hard-bitten blonde who is removed from prison to testify in the deportation trial of a notorious gangster. The last of the state's witnesses, since the others have been extinguished in gangland style, she is sequestered in a hotel suite for a weekend while awaiting her testimony, guarded by a detective (Brian Keith), a prosecutor (Edward G. Robinson), and a

*Her television debut, also in 1954, came on *Producer's Showcase* on NBC in an Otto Preminger-directed version of Noel Coward's *Tonight at 8:30*. She appeared in three of his nine playlets—*Red Peppers, Still Life,* and *Shadow Play*—with a cast that included Trevor Howard, Gig Young and Martyn Green. Her own special, *The Ginger Rogers Show,* with Ray Bolger and the Ritz Brothers, was broadcast on CBS in 1958. A pilot for a half-hour variety show bearing her name did not attract sponsors in 1959. She appeared frequently on television throughout the sixties, and continues to, less frequently, today.

TWIST OF FATE (1954). With Stanley Baker

TIGHT SPOT (1955). With Joseph Hamilton and Edward G. Robinson

prison matron (Katherine Anderson). As must be expected of such a character, she discloses her "framed" past; but the real shock is that the detective assigned to protect her is also on the crime czar's payroll. While the story ticks away to its melodramatic conclusion, a televised hillbilly program lends a satirical counterpoint to the narrative. The cast for this modest thriller, is exceptional. Edward G. Robinson, never spiritless, is a suitable attorney; Keith is impressive as the thug-cop who falls in love with his victim; Lorne Greene is sinister as the bigwig mobster; and Eve McVeagh, as Rogers' sister, was good in a bitter reunion scene. Rogers herself, whose role was scarcely a departure from her past, complemented her meager surroundings.

Arthur Lubin, who piloted the "Francis, the Talking Mule" series, was culpable for the catastrophe of *The First Traveling Saleslady,* a movie which had the dubious distinction of celebrating Rogers' return to enfeebled RKO after ten

THE FIRST TRAVELING SALESLADY (1956). With Carol Channing

years elsewhere. Carol Channing, who avoided the screen for years afterward, also made her debut in this stale, prefabricated and remotely feminist vehicle. The comedy concerned the exploits of a staunch saleswoman (Rogers) who markets corsets in the Old West of the Gay Nineties. Rogers attempts to salvage her dying corset biz by expanding to barbed wire in Texas, even though previous barbed-wire merchants have dangled at the end of a rope by courtesy of free-range fanatics. In this bald-faced burlesque, she encounters bargain-store "Injuns," the Prince of Wales, "Teddy Roosevelt" (played by Edward Cassidy) and a host of typical Western japes, all unintelligent and deadly. Channing is her sidekick, and she croons "A Corset Can Do A Lot For A Lady" as her sole contribution. Rogers, who flaunts a harsh nasal twang, is dominated by the script, indeed by several "tall men" recruited from television programs of the day, including Barry Nelson, David Brian, and James Arness. Even Clint Eastwood is lurking in the background. Lame, offbeat, an interesting but failed experiment, *The First Traveling Saleslady* only underlined the emptiness of such backward-looking fare in changing times.

Her last fling at true artistry, three more credits notwithstanding, was *Teenage Rebel,* smoothly directed by Edmund Goulding for Twentieth Century-Fox in 1956. The movie, in CinemaScope, was scripted by Walter Reisch and Charles Brackett (who also produced), based on the Broadway play, *A Roomful of Roses,* by Edith Sommer. The cinema title is a misnomer, however, for the story is not of the leather-jacket set, but rather that of a teen-aged girl who is reunited with her mother after a separation of eight years. Her father (John Stephenson) who had spirited her abroad after a divorce settlement eight years previous, now intends to remarry without informing his daughter. She arrives in California to visit Rogers, unaware of the conspiracy and hating her remarried mom. Her resolve is softened by neighboring teens (Warren Berlinger, from the Broadway cast, is especially winning as a dragstrip romeo) until she discovers that they have been "hired" by stepfather Michael Rennie to ease her stay. Then she erupts again, and flies cross-country back into the uncertain arms of father. Accompanied by mother Rogers, who is distraught over the prospect

TEENAGE REBEL (1956). With Betty Lou Keim

of losing her daughter once more, she perceives the real, unfeeling nature of her father's custody and, in an ending that is nicely delayed and unashamedly poignant, mother and daughter speed off in a taxi, eluding father's grasp and ending the movie in a flood of tears.

Teenage Rebel is a tolerable coda to her career, the last fair look at Ginger Rogers on the screen, tasteful, insightful, and balancing the urge toward sentimentality with a dose of civility. It is a soap opera, yes, with an idealized view of California suburbia, specifically Palo Alto: a life replete with black servants, teen-agers who gulp milk, carefree malt shop afternoons, and crucial weekend hot-rod races. But the cast (excepting Betty Lou Keim, reprising her Broadway part as the mannered, insecure daughter) is thankfully restrained. And Rogers is particularly earnest, precisely capturing the torn emotions of a mother who cannot "reach" her daughter and who must watch helplessly as the lonely teenager withdraws into an imagined world without friends. She plays the opening reel in tennis shorts—looking, as always, incredibly prime—and though her performance is a touch off-key in moments, it is ultimately quite stirring. She proved, even as her stardom plummeted, that she was capable of conjuring class from trash.

Nunnally Johnson, the writer-

OH MEN! OH WOMEN! (1957). With Dan Dailey and David Niven

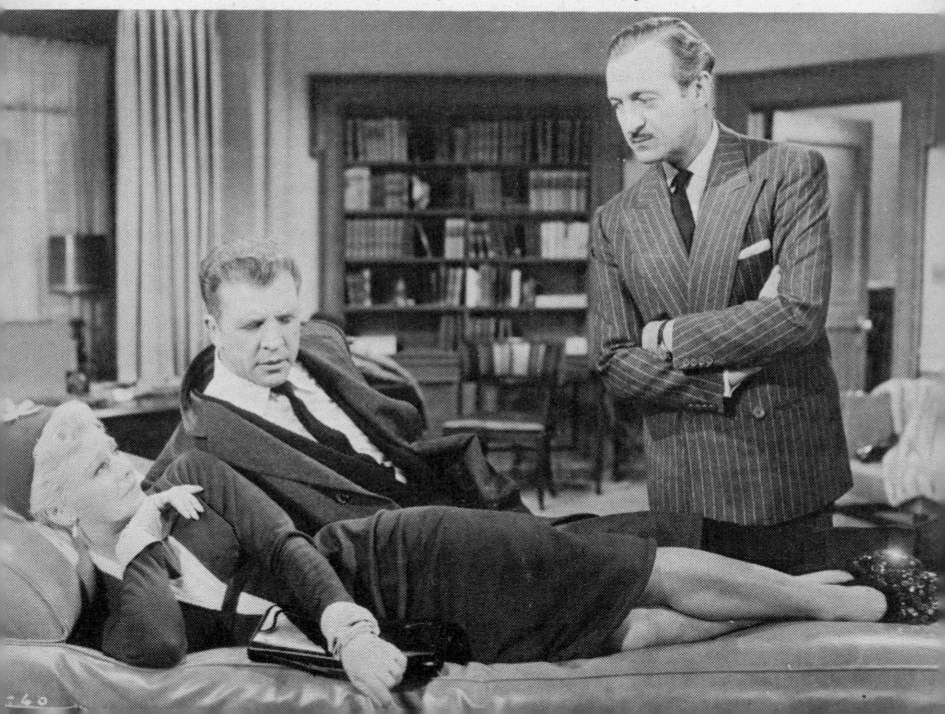

HARLOW (1965). With Carol Lynley

director of *Black Widow,* also adapted and directed Edward Chodorov's play, *Oh Men! Oh Women!* for Fox in 1957, resulting in a bird-brained comedy with distressingly few virtues. Rogers withered into a cast which included Tony Randall (then a newcomer, fresh from television as Wally Cox's tagalong in *Mr. Peepers*), David Niven, Dan Dailey, and Barbara Rush. The story, which begins with a rambling Tony Randall monologue on the psychiatric couch, was a tin parody of the shrink profession and centers on a well-ordered psychiatrist (Niven) whose life crumbles at the intrusion of some wacky patients. One such is his own fiancée (Barbara Rush) who, it is discovered, has been moonlighting as Tony Randall's girlfriend. Rogers, meanwhile, is the wife of movie star Dan Dailey, and she is simply bored with housewifery, as, despite the valiant efforts of the cast, moviegoers were likely to be bored with the entire business. Richard Corliss has accurately characterized Nunnally Johnson's films of the fifties as tending "to slouch, then droop, then amiably fall asleep."

The actress never regained any momentum and, in fact, was idle after *Oh Men! Oh Women!* for

THE CONFESSION (1964). With Michael Ansara and Barbara Eden (extreme right)

nearly eight years. She busied herself with night-club work, stock theater work, and even, in 1959, a pre-Broadway bound comedy entitled *The Pink Jungle,* about the cosmetics industry, which folded ingloriously in Boston en route to New York City. A rumor circulated that friction had erupted between mama Lela Rogers, still in her daughter's entourage, and Agnes Moorehead, the other female principal. It wasn't until 1965 that Rogers made her comeback, and then only as the substitute for an ailing Judy Garland in the Electronovision version of *Harlow.** She played the mother of "platinum blonde" Jean Harlow. Directed by Alex Segal in just eight days, a quickie schedule that put the film in release weeks before Joseph E. Levine's production on Harlow, the movie was catchpenny and sensationalistic, atrociously scripted, focusing on Harlow's ill-fated marriage and untimely death. It was the third (preceded by *Hamlet* and *The T.A.M.I. Story*) movie in the short-lived and grainy Electronovision process, and its technical standards were shoddy. Besides a lackluster title performance by Carol Lynley, the project was hampered by such miscasting as Jack Kruschen as an amiable Louis B. Mayer, Efrem Zimbalist, Jr., as a combination William Powell and Clark Gable, Hermione Baddeley as Marie Dressler, and John Williams as the enigmatic Howard Hughes. As for Rogers, she was indescribably raunchy, either the best or worst thing in the movie, depending on which opinion of the split verdict is finally true. *The New York Times* liked her whiny, pushy characterization, for example, while *Variety* sniffed, "Miss Rogers is lost in her role."

Actually, her parting shot, a movie called *The Confession,* had only spotty showings; it was shot in 1964, as an independent venture in partnership with husband William Marshall, in Jamaica under the direction of William Dieterle. The Jamaican government offered the Rogers-Marshall team tax benefits to shoot on-location on the island, and there was brief talk in the press that the couple would switch their citizenship to the beckoning country. Their studio in Jamaica was later used for *Father Goose* and *High Wind in Jamaica,* but the company itself was soon disbanded by a disillusioned Rogers. In the cast of *The Confession* are Ray Milland, Barbara Eden, and Elliott Gould as a deaf mute. Rogers, in a dark wig, played the madam of an Italian bordello but, even today, she dismisses the movie curtly as a "terrible" film.

*That year she appeared on stage as Dolly Levi (one of a number of replacements for the original Carol Channing) in the musical *Hello, Dolly!*

Ginger and Fred reunited at MGM's party for THAT'S ENTERTAINMENT! (1974)

The Confession received meager release in the seventies as *Seven Different Ways* before being sold to television, where it was given another title, *Quick, Let's Get Married.* But it is a rare and intriguing item, and, literally, the career of Ginger Rogers lacks its definitive terminus.

Whatever the vague nature of her last film to date, she remains vividly alive for moviegoers. More than four decades have passed since she made her debut, but her image endures: independent, down-to-earth, spunky, and forever glamorous in blue jeans or satin gown. No matter the passage of time. She is a memory that extends beyond the years, beyond the movies, into the collective soul of a nation.

BIBLIOGRAPHY

Astaire, Fred, *Steps in Time,* New York: Harper, 1959.

Chierichetti, David, *Hollywood Director,* New York: Curtis, 1973.

Croce, Arlene, *The Fred Astaire & Ginger Rogers Book,* New York: Outerbridge & Lazard, 1972.

"Dancing Girl," *Time,* April 10, 1939.

"Dancing with Astaire and Rogers," *Literary Digest,* December 12, 1936.

Dickens, Homer, "Ginger Rogers," *Films in Review,* March, 1966.

Ferguson, Otis, *The Film Criticism of Otis Ferguson,* Philadelphia: Temple University Press, 1971.

Haskell, Molly, *From Reverence to Rape: The Treatment of Women in the Movies,* New York: Holt, Rinehart and Winston, 1973.

Kanin, Garson, *Hollywood,* New York: Viking, 1974.

Parish, James Robert, *The RKO Gals,* New Rochelle: Arlington House, 1974.

Rosen, Marjorie, *Popcorn Venus,* New York: Coward, McCann and Geoghegan, 1973.

Sennett, Ted, *Lunatics and Lovers,* New Rochelle: Arlington House, 1974.

"She Adds New Chapter . . . ," *Life,* March 2, 1942.

Shearer, Lloyd, "One of the World's Most Fascinating Women," *Parade,* April 9, 1961.

Shipman, David, *The Great Movie Stars: The Golden Years,* New York: Crown, 1970.

Shipp, Cameron, "How to Dance Like Four Antelopes," *Colliers,* January 8, 1949.

THE FILMS OF GINGER ROGERS

The director's name follows the release date. A (c) following the release date indicates that the film was in color. Sp indicates screenplay and b/o indicates based on.

1. YOUNG MAN OF MANHATTAN. Paramount, 1930. *Monta Bell.* Sp: Robert Presnell, b/o novel by Katharine Brush. Cast: Norman Foster, Claudette Colbert, Charles Ruggles, Leslie Austin, H. Dudley Hawley.

2. QUEEN HIGH. Paramount, 1930. *Fred Newmeyer.* Sp: Frank Mandel, b/o play by Laurence Schwab, B. G. DeSylva, and Lewis Gensler, plus play *A Pair of Sixes* by Edward Henry Peple. Cast: Frank Morgan, Charles Ruggles, Stanley Smith, Helen Carrington, Theresa Maxwell Conover, Betty Garde, Nina Olivette, Rudy Cameron, Tom Brown.

3. THE SAP FROM SYRACUSE. Paramount, 1930. *A. Edward Sutherland.* Sp: Gertrude Purcell, b/o play by John Wray, Jack O'Donnell, and John Hayden. Cast: Jack Oakie, Granville Bates, George Barbier, Sidney Riggs, Betty Starbuck, Verree Teasdale, J. Malcolm Dunn.

4. FOLLOW THE LEADER. Paramount, 1930. *Norman Taurog.* Sp: Gertrude Purcell, b/o play *Manhattan Mary* by William K. Wells, George White, B. G. De Sylva, Lew Brown, and Ray Henderson. Cast: Ed Wynn, Stanley Smith, Lou Holtz, Lida Kane, Ethel Merman, Bobby Watson, William Halligan, Preston Foster, William Gargan, Jack La Rue.

5. HONOR AMONG LOVERS. Paramount, 1931. *Dorothy Arzner.* Sp: Austin Parker, b/o his story. Cast: Claudette Colbert, Fredric March, Monroe Owsley, Charles Ruggles, Avonne Taylor, Pat O'Brien, Janet McLeay, John Kearney, Ralph Morgan.

6. THE TIP OFF. RKO-Pathé, 1931. *Albert Rogell.* Sp: Lew Lipton, b/o story by George Kibbe Turner. Cast: Eddie Quillan, Robert Armstrong, Joan Peers, Ralf Harolde, Charles Sellon, Mike Donlin.

7. SUICIDE FLEET. RKO-Pathé, 1931. *Albert Rogell.* Sp: Lew Lipton, b/o story by Commander Herbert A. Jones. Cast: Bill Boyd, Robert Armstrong, James Gleason, Harry Bannister, Frank Reicher, Ben Alexander, Henry Victor.

8. CARNIVAL BOAT. RKO, 1932. *Albert Rogell.* Sp: James Seymour, b/o story by Marion Jackson and Don Ryan. Cast: Bill Boyd, Fred Kohler, Hobart Bosworth, Marie Prevost, Edgar Kennedy, Harry Sweet, Charles Sellon.

9. THE TENDERFOOT. First National, 1932. *Ray Enright*. Sp: Arthur Caesar, Monty Banks, and Earl Baldwin, b/o play *The Butter and Egg Man* by George S. Kaufman. Cast: Joe E. Brown, Lew Cody, Vivian Oakland, Robert Grieg, Wilfred Lucas, Spencer Charters, Ralph Ince, Mae Madison, Marion Byron. Also filmed in 1928, 1940, and 1953.

10. THE THIRTEENTH GUEST. Monogram, 1932. *Albert Ray*. Sp: Francis Hyland, Arthur Hoerl, Armitage Trail, b/o novel by Trail. Cast: Lyle Talbot, J. Farrell MacDonald, James Eagles, Eddie Phillips, Erville Alderson, Robert Klein, Crauford Kent, Brandon Hurst. Remade in 1943 as *The Mystery of the 13th Guest*.

11. HAT CHECK GIRL. Fox, 1932. *Sidney Lanfield*. Sp: Philip Klein, Barry Conners, and Arthur Kober, b/o novel by Rian James. Cast: Sally Eilers, Ben Lyon, Monroe Owsley, Arthur Pierson, Noel Madison, Dewey Robinson, Harold Goodwin.

12. YOU SAID A MOUTHFUL. First National, 1932. *Lloyd Bacon*. Sp: Robert Lord, Bolton Mallory, b/o story by William B. Dover. Cast: Joe E. Brown, Preston Foster, Sheila Terry, Guinn Williams, Harry Gribbon, Farina, Oscar Apfel, Edwin Maxwell, Walter Walker.

13. 42nd STREET. Warner Brothers, 1933. *Lloyd Bacon*. Sp: James Seymour and Rian James, b/o novel by Bradford Ropes. Cast: Warner Baxter, Bebe Daniels, George Brent, Una Merkel, Ruby Keeler, Guy Kibbee, Ned Sparks, Dick Powell, Allen Jenkins, Henry B. Walthall, George E. Stone.

14. BROADWAY BAD. Fox, 1933. *Sidney Lanfield*. Sp: Arthur Kober and Maude Fulton, b/o story by William R. Lipman and A. W. Pezet. Cast: Joan Blondell, Ricardo Cortez, Adrienne Ames, Allen Vincent, Victor Jory, Philip Tead, Francis McDonald, Spencer Charters, Donald Crisp.

15. GOLD DIGGERS OF 1933. Warner Brothers, 1933. *Mervyn LeRoy*. Sp: Erwin Gelsey, James Seymour, David Boehm, and Ben Markson, b/o play *The Gold Diggers* by Avery Hopwood. Cast: Warren William, Joan Blondell, Aline MacMahon, Ruby Keeler, Dick Powell, Guy Kibbee, Ned Sparks, Sterling Holloway, Ferdinand Gottschalk, Billy Barty.

16. PROFESSIONAL SWEETHEART. RKO, 1933. *William A. Seiter*. Sp: Maurine Watkins. Cast: Norman Foster, ZaSu Pitts, Frank McHugh, Allen Jenkins, Gregory Ratoff, Edgar Kennedy, Lucien Littlefield, Franklin Pangborn, Betty Furness.

17. A SHRIEK IN THE NIGHT. Allied, 1933. *Albert Ray*. Sp: Frances Hyland, b/o story by Kurt Kempler. Cast: Lyle Talbot, Arthur Hoyt, Purnell Pratt, Harvey Clark, Lillian Harmer, Maurice Black, Louise Beavers, Clarence Wilson.

18. DON'T BET ON LOVE. Universal, 1933. *Murray Roth.* Sp: Howard E. Rogers, Ben Ryan, and Roth. Cast: Lew Ayres, Charles Grapewin, Shirley Grey, Merna Kennedy, Thomas Dugan, Robert Emmett O'Connor, Lucille Webster Gleason.

19. SITTING PRETTY. Paramount, 1933. *Harry Joe Brown.* Sp: Jack McGowan, S. J. Perelman, and Lou Breslow, b/o story by Nina Wilcox Putnam. Cast: Jack Oakie, Jack Haley, Thelma Todd, Gregory Ratoff, Lew Cody, Harry Revel, Jerry Tucker, Mack Gordon.

20. FLYING DOWN TO RIO. RKO, 1933. *Thornton Freeland.* Sp: Cyril Hume, H. W. Hanemann, and Erwin Gelsey, b/o story by Lou Brock, from play by Anne Caldwell. Cast: Dolores Del Rio, Gene Raymond, Raul Roulien, Fred Astaire, Blanche Frederici, Walter Walker, Etta Moten, Eric Blore, Franklin Pangborn, Luis Alberni.

21. CHANCE AT HEAVEN. RKO, 1933. *William A. Seiter.* Sp: Julian Josephson and Sarah Y. Mason, b/o story by Viña Delmar. Cast: Joel McCrea, Marion Nixon, Andy Devine, Virginia Hammond, Lucien Littlefield, Ann Shoemaker, George Meeker, Betty Furness, Herman Bing.

22. RAFTER ROMANCE. RKO, 1934. *William A. Seiter.* Sp: H. W. Hanemann, Sam Mintz, and Glenn Tryon, b/o story by John Wells. Cast: Norman Foster, George Sidney, Robert Benchley, Laura Hope Crews, Guinn Williams.

23. FINISHING SCHOOL. RKO, 1934. *Wanda Tuchock and George Nicholls, Jr.* Sp: Tuchock and Laird Doyle, b/o story by David Hempstead. Cast: Frances Dee, Billie Burke, Bruce Cabot, John Halliday, Beulah Bondi, Sara Haden, Marjorie Lytell, Adalyn Doyle, Dawn O'Day (Anne Shirley).

24. 20 MILLION SWEETHEARTS. First National, 1934. *Ray Enright.* Sp: Warren Duff and Harry Sauber, b/o story by Paul Finder Moss and Jerry Wald. Cast: Pat O'Brien, Dick Powell, Allen Jenkins, Grant Mitchell, Joseph Cawthorn, Joan Wheeler, Henry O'Neill.

25. CHANGE OF HEART. Fox, 1934. *John G. Blystone.* Sp: Sonya Levien, James Gleason, and Samuel Hoffenstein, b/o novel *Manhattan Love Song* by Kathleen Norris. Cast: Janet Gaynor, Charles Farrell, James Dunn, Beryl Mercer, Gustav von Seyffertitz, Irene Franklin, Kenneth Thomson, Theodor von Eltz, Shirley Temple.

26. UPPER WORLD. Warner Brothers, 1934. *Roy Del Ruth.* Sp: Ben Markson, b/o story by Ben Hecht. Cast: Warren William, Mary Astor, Andy Devine, Dickie Moore, Henry O'Neill, J. Carrol Naish, Sidney Toler, Theodore Newton, Robert Barrat, Ferdinand Gottschalk, John Qualen.

27. THE GAY DIVORCEE. RKO, 1934. *Mark Sandrich.* Sp: George Marion Jr., Dorothy Yost, and Edward Kaufman, b/o musical play *Gay Divorce,* book by Dwight Taylor, adapted musically by Kenneth Webb and Samuel Hoffenstein. Cast: Fred Astaire, Alice Brady, Edward Everett Horton, Erik Rhodes, Eric Blore, Lillian Miles, Charles Coleman, William Austin, Betty Grable, Paul Porcasi, E. E. Clive.

28. ROMANCE IN MANHATTAN. RKO, 1934. *Stephen Roberts.* Sp: Jane Murfin and Edward Kaufman, b/o story by Norman Krasna and Don Hartman. Cast: Francis Lederer, Arthur Hohl, Jimmy Butler, J. Farrell MacDonald, Helen Ware, Eily Malyon, Lillian Harmer, Donald Meek, Sidney Toler.

29. ROBERTA. RKO, 1935. *William A. Seiter.* Sp: Jane Murfin, Sam Mintz, Allan Scott, and Glenn Tryon, b/o musical play *Roberta,* book by Otto Harbach, which was based on Alice Duer Miller's novel *Gowns by Roberta.* Cast: Irene Dunne, Fred Astaire, Randolph Scott, Helen Westley, Claire Dodd, Victor Varconi, Luis Alberni, Ferdinand Munier, Torben Meyer. Remade in 1952 as *Lovely to Look At.*

30. STAR OF MIDNIGHT. RKO, 1935. *Stephen Roberts.* Sp: Howard J. Green, Anthony Veiller, and Edward Kaufman, b/o novel by Arthur Somers Roche. Cast: William Powell, Paul Kelly, Gene Lockhart, Ralph Morgan, Leslie Fenton, J. Farrell MacDonald, Russell Hopton, Vivian Oakland.

31. TOP HAT. RKO, 1935. *Mark Sandrich.* Sp: Dwight Taylor and Allan Scott, b/o story by Taylor. Cast: Fred Astaire, Edward Everett Horton, Erik Rhodes, Eric Blore, Helen Broderick, Edgar Norton, Gino Corrado, Leonard Mudie, Lucille Ball.

32. IN PERSON. RKO, 1935. *William A. Seiter.* Sp: Allan Scott, b/o novel by Samuel Hopkins Adams. Cast: George Brent, Alan Mowbray, Grant Mitchell, Samuel S. Hinds, Joan Breslau, Louis Mason, Spencer Charters, Edgar Kennedy.

33. FOLLOW THE FLEET. RKO, 1936. *Mark Sandrich.* Sp: Dwight Taylor and Allan Scott, b/o play *Shore Leave* by Hubert Osborne. Cast: Fred Astaire, Randolph Scott, Harriet Hilliard, Astrid Allwyn, Harry Beresford, Russell Hicks, Brooks Benedict, Ray Mayer, Lucille Ball, Betty Grable, Joy Hodges. Also filmed in 1925, 1930, and 1955.

34. SWING TIME. RKO, 1936. *George Stevens.* Sp: Howard Lindsay and Allan Scott, b/o story by Erwin Gelsey. Cast: Fred Astaire, Victor Moore, Helen Broderick, Eric Blore, Georges Metaxa, Betty Furness, Landers Stevens, John Harrington, Pierre Watkin.

35. SHALL WE DANCE. RKO, 1937. *Mark Sandrich.* Sp: Allan Scott, Ernest Pagano, and P. J. Wolfson, b/o story by Lee Loeb and Harold Buchman. Cast:

Fred Astaire, Edward Everett Horton, Eric Blore, Jerome Cowan, Ketti Gallian, William Brisbane, Frank Moran, Ann Shoemaker, Harriet Hoctor.

36. STAGE DOOR. RKO, 1937. *Gregory La Cava.* Sp: Morrie Ryskind and Anthony Veiller, b/o play by Edna Ferber and George S. Kaufman. Cast: Katharine Hepburn, Adolphe Menjou, Gail Patrick, Constance Collier, Andrea Leeds, Samuel S. Hinds, Lucille Ball, Franklin Pangborn, Grady Sutton, Eve Arden, Ann Miller, Margaret Early, Jack Carson.

37. HAVING WONDERFUL TIME. RKO, 1938. *Alfred Santell.* Sp: Arthur Kober, b/o his play. Cast: Douglas Fairbanks, Jr., Peggy Conklin, Lucille Ball, Lee Bowman, Eve Arden, Dorothea Kent, Richard "Red" Skelton, Ann Miller, Donald Meek, Jack Carson, Grady Sutton.

38. VIVACIOUS LADY. RKO, 1938. *George Stevens.* Sp: P. J. Wolfson and Ernest Pagano, b/o story by I.A.R. Wylie. Cast: James Stewart, James Ellison, Beulah Bondi, Charles Coburn, Frances Mercer, Phyllis Kennedy, Franklin Pangborn, Grady Sutton, Jack Carson, Alec Craig, Willie Best, Hattie McDaniel.

39. CAREFREE. RKO, 1938. *Mark Sandrich.* Sp: Allan Scott, Ernest Pagano, Dudley Nichols, and Hagar Wilde. Cast: Fred Astaire, Ralph Bellamy, Luella Gear, Jack Carson, Clarence Kolb, Franklin Pangborn, Walter Kingsford, Kay Sutton, Tom Tully, Hattie McDaniel, Robert B. Mitchell.

40. THE STORY OF VERNON AND IRENE CASTLE. RKO, 1939. *H. C. Potter.* Sp: Richard Sherman, Oscar Hammerstein II, and Dorothy Yost, b/o stories *My Husband* and *My Memories of Vernon Castle* by Irene Castle. Cast: Fred Astaire, Edna May Oliver, Walter Brennan, Lew Fields, Etienne Girardot, Rolfe Sedan, Janet Beecher, Robert Strange, Leonid Kinskey, Clarence Derwent, Victor Varconi, Frances Mercer, Donald MacBride.

41. BACHELOR MOTHER. RKO, 1939. *Garson Kanin.* Sp: Norman Krasna, b/o story by Felix Jackson. Cast: David Niven, Charles Coburn, Frank Albertson, E. E. Clive, Elbert Coplen, Jr., Ferike Boros, Ernest Truex, Leonard Penn. Remade in 1956 as *Bundle of Joy.*

42. FIFTH AVENUE GIRL. RKO, 1939. *Gregory La Cava.* Sp: Allan Scott. Cast: Walter Connolly, Verree Teasdale, James Ellison, Tim Holt, Kathryn Adams, Franklin Pangborn, Cornelius Keefe, Ferike Boros, Louis Calhern, Jack Carson.

43. PRIMROSE PATH. RKO, 1940. *Gregory La Cava.* Sp: Allan Scott and La Cava, b/o play by Robert L. Buckner, Walter Hart and novel *February Hill* by Victoria Lincoln. Cast: Joel McCrea, Marjorie Rambeau, Henry Travers, Miles Mander, Queenie Vassar, Joan Carroll, Vivienne Osborne, Carmen Morales.

44. LUCKY PARTNERS. RKO, 1940. *Lewis Milestone*. Sp: Allan Scott and John Van Druten, b/o story *Bonne Chance* by Sacha Guitry. Cast: Ronald Colman, Jack Carson, Spring Byington, Cecilia Loftus, Harry Davenport, Hugh O'Connell, Brandon Tynan, Leon Belasco, Eddie Conrad, Walter Kingsford, Lucille Gleason.

45. KITTY FOYLE. RKO, 1940. *Sam Wood*. Sp: Dalton Trumbo and Donald Ogden Stewart, b/o novel by Christopher Morley. Cast: Dennis Morgan, James Craig, Eduardo Ciannelli, Ernest Cossart, Gladys Cooper, Odette Myrtil, Mary Treen, Katharine Stevens, Walter Kingsford, Cecil Cunningham, Nella Walker.

46. TOM, DICK AND HARRY. RKO, 1941. *Garson Kanin*. Sp: Paul Jarrico. Cast: George Murphy, Alan Marshal, Burgess Meredith, Joe Cunningham, Jane Seymour, Lenore Lonergan, Vicki Lester, Phil Silvers, Betty Breckenridge, Sid Skolsky. Remade in 1958 as *The Girl Most Likely*.

47. ROXIE HART. Twentieth Century-Fox 1942. *William A. Wellman*. Sp: Nunnally Johnson, b/o play *Chicago* by Maurine Watkins. Cast: Adolphe Menjou, George Montgomery, Lynne Overman, Nigel Bruce, Phil Silvers, Sara Allgood, William Frawley, Spring Byington. Also filmed in 1927.

48. TALES OF MANHATTAN. Twentieth Century-Fox, 1942. *Julien Duvivier*. Sp: Ben Hecht, Ferenc Molnar, Donald Ogden Stewart, Samuel Hoffenstein, Alan Campbell, Ladislas Fodor, Laslo Vadnay, Laszlo Gorog, Lamar Trotti, and Henry Blankfort. Cast: Charles Boyer, Rita Hayworth, Henry Fonda, Charles Laughton, Edward G. Robinson, Paul Robeson, Ethel Waters, Eddie (Rochester) Anderson, Thomas Mitchell, Eugene Pallette, Cesar Romero, Gail Patrick, Roland Young.

49. THE MAJOR AND THE MINOR. Paramount, 1942. *Billy Wilder*. Sp: Charles Brackett and Wilder, b/o play *Connie Goes Home* by Edward Childs Carpenter and story *Sunny Goes Home* by Fannie Kilbourne. Cast: Ray Milland, Rita Johnson, Robert Benchley, Diana Lynn, Edward Fielding, Frankie Thomas, Jr., Raymond Roe, Charles Smith, Lela Rogers. Remade in 1955 as *You're Never Too Young*.

50. ONCE UPON A HONEYMOON. RKO, 1942. *Leo McCarey*. Sp: Sheridan Gibney, b/o story by McCarey and Gibney. Cast: Cary Grant, Walter Slezak, Albert Dekker, Albert Basserman, Ferike Boros, Harry Shannon, John Banner, Natasha Lytess, Alex Melesh.

51. TENDER COMRADE. RKO, 1943. *Edward Dmytryk*. Sp: Dalton Trumbo. Cast: Robert Ryan, Ruth Hussey, Patricia Collinge, Mady Christians, Kim Hunter, Jane Darwell, Mary Forbes, Richard Martin.

52. LADY IN THE DARK. Paramount, 1944 (c). *Mitchell Leisen.* Sp: Frances Goodrich and Albert Hackett, b/o play by Moss Hart, Kurt Weill, and Ira Gershwin. Cast: Ray Milland, Jon Hall, Warner Baxter, Barry Sullivan, Mischa Auer, Mary Philips, Phyllis Brooks, Edward Fielding, Gail Russell.

53. I'LL BE SEEING YOU. A David O. Selznick Production, released by United Artists, 1944. *William Dieterle.* Sp: Marion Parsonnet, b/o radio play by Charles Martin. Cast: Joseph Cotten, Shirley Temple, Spring Byington, Tom Tully, Chill Wills, Dare Harris, Kenny Bowers, John Derek.

54. WEEKEND AT THE WALDORF. MGM, 1945. *Robert Z. Leonard.* Sp: Sam and Bella Spewack, Guy Bolton, b/o play *Grand Hotel* by Vicki Baum. Cast: Walter Pidgeon, Van Johnson, Lana Turner, Robert Benchley, Edward Arnold, Constance Collier, Leon Ames, Warner Anderson, Phyllis Thaxter, Keenan Wynn, Xavier Cugat, Lina Romay. A remake of *Grand Hotel.* (1932).

55. HEARTBEAT. RKO, 1946. *Sam Wood.* Sp: Hans Wilhelm, Max Kolpe, Michel Duran, Morrie Ryskind, and Rowland Leigh, Cast: Jean Pierre Aumont, Adolphe Menjou, Basil Rathbone, Eduardo Ciannelli, Mikhail Rasumny, Melville Cooper, Mona Maris, Henry Stephenson.

56. MAGNIFICENT DOLL. Universal, 1946. *Frank Borzage.* Sp: Irving Stone. Cast: David Niven, Burgess Meredith, Stephen McNally, Peggy Wood, Frances Williams, Robert Barrat, Grandon Rhodes.

57. IT HAD TO BE YOU. Columbia, 1947. *Don Hartman,* and *Rudolph Maté.* Sp: Norman Panama and Melvin Frank, b/o story by Hartman and Allen Boretz. Cast: Cornel Wilde, Percy Waram, Spring Byington, Ron Randell, Thurston Hall, Charles Evans.

58. THE BARKLEYS OF BROADWAY. MGM, 1949 (c). *Charles Walters.* Sp: Betty Comden and Adolph Green. Cast: Fred Astaire, Oscar Levant, Billie Burke, Gale Robbins, Jacques François, George Zucco, Clinton Sundberg, Hans Conreid.

59. PERFECT STRANGERS. Warner Brothers, 1950. *Bretaigne Windust.* Sp: Edith Sommer and George Oppenheimer, b/o play *Ladies and Gentlemen* by Charles MacArthur and Ben Hecht. Cast: Dennis Morgan, Thelma Ritter, Margalo Gillmore, Anthony Ross, Howard Freeman, Alan Reed, Paul Ford, Harry Bellaver.

60. STORM WARNING. Warner Brothers, 1951. *Stuart Heisler.* Sp: Daniel Fuchs and Richard Brooks. Cast: Ronald Reagan, Doris Day, Steve Cochran, Hugh Sanders, Lloyd Gough, Raymond Greenleaf, Ned Glass, Paul E. Burns, Walter Baldwin, Lynn Whitney.

61. THE GROOM WORE SPURS. A Fidelity Pictures Production, released by Universal-International, 1951. *Richard Whorf.* Sp: Robert Carson, Robert Libott, Frank Burt, b/o story *Legal Bride* by Carson. Cast: Jack Carson, Joan Davis, Stanley Ridges, James Brown, John Litel, Victor Sen Yung, Mira McKinney.

62. WE'RE NOT MARRIED. Twentieth Century-Fox, 1952. *Edmund Goulding.* Sp: Nunnally Johnson and Dwight Taylor, b/o story by Gina Kaus and Jay Dratler. Cast: Fred Allen, Victor Moore, Marilyn Monroe, David Wayne, Eve Arden, Paul Douglas, Eddie Bracken, Mitzi Gaynor, Louis Calhern, Zsa Zsa Gabor, James Gleason.

63. MONKEY BUSINESS. Twentieth Century-Fox, 1952. *Howard Hawks.* Sp: Ben Hecht, Charles Lederer, and I.A.L. Diamond, b/o story by Harry Segall. Cast: Cary Grant, Charles Coburn, Marilyn Monroe, Hugh Marlowe, Henri Letondal, Robert Cornthwaite, Larry Keating, Douglas Spencer, Esther Dale, George Winslow, Harry Carey, Jr.

64. DREAMBOAT. Twentieth Century-Fox, 1952. *Claude Binyon.* Sp: Binyon, b/o story by John D. Weaver. Cast: Clifton Webb, Anne Francis, Jeffrey Hunter, Elsa Lanchester, Fred Clark, Paul Harvey, Ray Collins.

65. FOREVER FEMALE. Paramount, 1953. *Irving Rapper.* Sp: Julius J. and Philip G. Epstein, b/o play *Rosalind* by J. M. Barrie. Cast: William Holden, Paul Douglas, Pat Crowley, James Gleason, Jesse White, Marjorie Rambeau, George Reeves, King Donovan.

66. BLACK WIDOW. Twentieth Century-Fox, 1954 (c). *Nunnally Johnson.* Sp: Johnson, b/o story by Patrick Quentin. Cast: Van Heflin, Gene Tierney, George Raft, Peggy Ann Garner, Reginald Gardiner, Virginia Leith, Otto Kruger, Cathleen Nesbitt, Skip Homeier, Hilda Simms.

67. TWIST OF FATE. A British Lion Film, released by United Artists, 1954. *David Miller.* Sp: Robert Westerby and Carl Nystrom, b/o story by Rip Van Ronkel. Cast: Herbert Lom, Jacques Bergerac, Stanley Baker, Margaret Rawlings, Eddie Byrne, Lily Kann, Coral Browne.

68. TIGHT SPOT. Columbia, 1955. *Phil Karlson.* Sp: William Bowers, b/o play *Dead Pigeon* by Lenard Kantor. Cast: Brian Keith, Edward G. Robinson, Katherine Anderson, Lorne Greene, Eve McVeagh, Allen Nourse, Peter Leeds, Lucy Marlow.

69. THE FIRST TRAVELING SALESLADY. RKO, 1956 (c). *Arthur Lubin.* Sp: Devery Freeman and Stephen Longstreet. Cast: Barry Nelson, Carol Channing, David Brian, James Arness, Clint Eastwood, Frank Wilcox, Robert Simon.

70. TEENAGE REBEL. Twentieth Century-Fox, 1956. *Edmund Goulding*. Sp: Walter Reisch and Charles Brackett, b/o play *A Roomful of Roses* by Edith Sommer. Cast: Michael Rennie, Betty Lou Keim, Mildred Natwick, Rusty Swope, Lili Gentle, Louise Beavers, Irene Hervey, John Stephenson, Warren Berlinger, Diane Jergens.

71. OH MEN! OH WOMEN! Twentieth Century-Fox, 1957 (c). *Nunnally Johnson*. Sp: Johnson, b/o play by Edward Chodorov. Cast: Dan Dailey, David Niven, Barbara Rush, Tony Randall, Natalie Schafer, Rachel Stephens, John Wengraf, Charles Davis, Franklin Pangborn.

72. THE CONFESSION. Golden Eagle, 1964. *William Dieterle*. Sp: Allen Scott. Cast: Ray Milland, Barbara Eden, Carl Schell, Michael Ansara, Elliott Gould, Walter Abel, Vinton Hayworth, Cecil Kellaway.

73. HARLOW. A Bill Sargent Production, released by Magna, 1965. *Alex Segal*. Sp: Karl Tunberg, Cast: Carol Lynley, Barry Sullivan, Efrem Zimbalist, Jr., Lloyd Bochner, John Williams, Hurd Hatfield, Audrey Totter, Jack Kruschen, Michael Dante, Hermione Baddeley, Audrey Christie.

INDEX

ABOUT THE AUTHOR

Patrick McGilligan writes for *The Boston Globe.* He is also the author of a book on James Cagney, entitled *Cagney: The Actor as Auteur.*

ABOUT THE EDITOR

Ted Sennett is the author of *Warner Brothers Presents,* a tribute to the great Warners films of the thirties and forties, and of *Lunatics and Lovers,* on the long-vanished but well-remembered "screwball" comedies of the past. He is also the editor of *The Movie Buff's Book* and has written about films for magazines and newspapers. He lives in New Jersey with his wife and three children.